MY SISTER
ROSALIND FRANKLIN

Frontispiece: Rosalind, in the 1950s (photo Peter Fisher).

MY SISTER
ROSALIND
FRANKLIN

⚬⚬⚬

JENIFER GLYNN

OXFORD
UNIVERSITY PRESS

OXFORD

UNIVERSITY PRESS

Great Clarendon Street, Oxford OX2 6DP

Oxford University Press is a department of the University of Oxford.
It furthers the University's objective of excellence in research, scholarship,
and education by publishing worldwide in

Oxford New York

Auckland Cape Town Dar es Salaam Hong Kong Karachi
Kuala Lumpur Madrid Melbourne Mexico City Nairobi
New Delhi Shanghai Taipei Toronto

With offices in

Argentina Austria Brazil Chile Czech Republic France Greece
Guatemala Hungary Italy Japan Poland Portugal Singapore
South Korea Switzerland Thailand Turkey Ukraine Vietnam

Oxford is a registered trade mark of Oxford University Press
in the UK and in certain other countries

Published in the United States
by Oxford University Press Inc., New York

British Library Cataloguing in Publication Data

Data available

Library of Congress Cataloging in Publication Data
Library of Congress Control Number: 2012931192

Typeset by SPI Publisher Services, Pondicherry, India
Printed in Great Britain
on acid-free paper by
Clays Ltd, St Ives plc

ISBN 978-0-19-969962-9

IN MEMORY OF OUR PARENTS,
ELLIS & MURIEL FRANKLIN

CONTENTS

LIST OF ILLUSTRATIONS

ACKNOWLEDGEMENTS

I could never have understood or written about Rosalind's science without the help of my husband, Ian, together with advice from Alan Windle, Nigel Unwin, and Ken Holmes. I am grateful to them, and to everyone who has read and criticized the manuscript: Aaron Klug, my brothers Colin and Roland Franklin, my children Sarah, Judith, and Simon, my grand-daughter Rebekah, and our friend Evi Wohlgemuth.

Thanks, too, to Jean Kerlogue for her memories; to Anne Sayre's publishers W. W. Norton for permission to quote from her interview with Raymond Gosling; and to the Wellcome Library for permission to quote Francis Crick's letter to James Watson, 13 April 1967.

I have had a great deal of kind cooperation over the illustrations, and I owe thanks to many people: to Quentin Blake for the use of two of the splendid drawings he made for the 'Cambridge 800' celebrations; to Peter Fisher for the use of his photographs of Rosalind, of our parents, and of our nanny; to my cousin Norman Franklin for supplying the photograph of Chartridge; to the librarian at St Paul's Girls' School and the archivist at Newnham College for photographs of the buildings; to my daughter Sarah for the photograph of 12 Mill Lane, and to my son Simon for the photographs of Rue Garancière and Avenue de la Motte

Picquet; to Vittorio Luzzati for the use of photographs of Rosalind on holiday in Tuscany and in the Alps; to the Royal Society of Chemistry for allowing the reproduction of the drawing of Rosalind's apparatus from the *Transactions of the Faraday Society*, vol. 45, 1949; and to the Medical Research Council Laboratory of Molecular Biology for the photograph of the model of the Tobacco Mosaic Virus. All other photographs are from my own collection.

All Rosalind's letters quoted are to our parents, except the few where the name of the recipient is given. They are all in my own collection.

I am very grateful to Latha Menon for encouraging me to write this book, and I should like to thank her, together with Emma Marchant and their colleagues at the Oxford University Press, for their help and support throughout.

PROLOGUE

Rosalind Franklin is famous in the history of science for her contribution to the discovery of the structure of DNA (deoxyribonucleic acid), which marked the start of the greatest biological revolution of the twentieth century. There has been endless discussion about the importance of her part, and about how her work was affected by her position as a woman scientist.

There have been other books—notably *Rosalind Franklin and DNA*, written by Anne Sayre in answer to James Watson's *The Double Helix*, and the full biography *Rosalind Franklin: The Dark Lady of DNA*, written by Brenda Maddox in 2002. The excuse for yet another book about Rosalind is that I am her sister. This naturally means that I may be biased, but it also means that I can tell her story in a family context, showing family reactions to her career, and her attitude to her family. I will try, with the help of her many letters, to give some idea of what she was like as a person. (Unless I say otherwise, all letters quoted are to our parents.)

Above all, of course, she was a distinguished scientist, not only in her work on DNA, but also in her earlier work on coals and carbons—still referred to by scientists in that field today—and in her later work on viruses. These three areas of work all connect, for they were all concerned with microstructures, first in physical materials and later in biological organisms. We, her family, never really understood what she was doing, only felt awe and pride.

She was not, as some have implied, totally committed to a life of nothing but science, with no outside interests, and prepared to give up all ideas of marriage and family. She had a great understanding of children and saw plenty of married women who managed to combine careers and families; she would have been more than happy to do the same herself but never found anyone she wanted to marry.

She had a great love of travel, and of mountains; her letters are full of her plans and accounts of her expeditions, and she enjoyed the company of those who could share her enthusiasm. She was prickly, did not make friends easily, but when she did she was outgoing and loyal. As my mother wrote, 'Her affections, both in childhood and in later life, were deep and strong and lasting, but she could never be demonstratively affectionate or readily express her deeper feelings in words.'

If she had not been a woman in a man's world, people often write, she might have achieved much more. Well, her problem was not that she was a woman, but that she did not have enough time. She died at thirty-seven, having written about twenty-one papers on carbons and about eighteen on viruses, as well as her classic papers on DNA.

CHAPTER I

Notting Hill

The underground railway line that served Notting Hill used to be called the Inner Circle. This gave the right atmosphere of enclosure. Now, more openly, it's the Circle Line, and the mixture of film, politicians, Carnival, and Portobello Market has made Notting Hill an unexpected focus for fame and tourism. The old local shops have disappeared, and little is left of the friendly district, with its many Anglo-Jewish families, that flourished between the wars.

Rosalind was born in Notting Hill, in Chepstow Villas, on 25 July 1920, joining her brother David who was fifteen months old. The move to nearby Pembridge Place came in 1923 when the family was growing—Colin in 1923, Roland in 1926, and finally myself, Jenifer, in 1929. My father had been born at 29 Pembridge Gardens, and the whole district was littered with Franklins.

My grandparents moved long before Rosalind was born, but only about a mile away to their parents' house, 35 Porchester Terrace, where they were joined, at no. 50, by Grandpa's brother

Ernest, married to his formidable cousin, the educationist and suffrage campaigner great-aunt Netta (Henrietta Montagu), and at no. 32 by Grandpa's sister Beatrice, married to her distinguished cousin Herbert Samuel, who became Home Secretary under Asquith and was to be the first High Commissioner of Mandate Palestine. That wasn't the lot. My father's elder brother Hugh was born at 28 Pembridge Villas, which must have been my grandparents' home before the grander Pembridge Gardens; Henry D'Arcy Hart (Netta's brother-in-law) was born in Pembridge Square and died at 18 Pembridge Gardens; the Waley Josephs (doubly cousins of ours) were in Linden Gardens; Netta herself, and her older siblings, were born in Lancaster Gate, the younger ones in Kensington Palace Gardens. I'm sure there were many more, but that will do for a start.

And, oddly as it seemed to us, not all Notting Hill Jews were related to Franklins. I remember Lazaruses in Pembridge Place, Goldings in Dawson Place, Levines within walking distance where my Austrian refugee companion Evi and I were sent for so-called Hebrew lessons.

My great-grandfather had been one of the founders of the New West End Synagogue, and I imagine this 'ghetto of Anglo-Jewry' had evolved so that we could all walk there on the Sabbath. But it no longer worked that way. Periodically my father went to the services regularly, but I think periodically also he lapsed. Certainly the centre of our childish life was The Park (Kensington Gardens) not the New West End. We often walked with our nanny (always known to us as Nannie) down Moscow Road and St Petersburgh Place (what was the Russian connection?) past the synagogue on our way to The Park.

We went, most days, in at the gate where the Balloon Lady sat selling lovely balloons and windmills, and on to the Round Pond. We would meet other nannies and children, and on special days might go as far as the 'flower walk' and the Albert Memorial, or the Dutch garden by Kensington Palace, or even 'the fountains' and the Peter Pan statue. On very special days the band might be playing and we would sit to listen, on seats (free) but never on deckchairs (twopence). It was such a closed society that when a new child and nanny appeared, the regulars muttered critically 'white gloves—must come from Hyde Park'. For we, in spite of our nanny-based upbringing, were consciously not posh, not white glove people. Some Franklin relatives might be presented at Court, but such fashionable frivolities were not for us.

The playground, now very smart and Princess Dianafied, was out of bounds in case we 'caught something'—I never knew what. But we loved the carved tree, and could touch all the little carved animals, now behind forbidding fencing. On the whole though, in spite of coaches in one corner and a café, the park is blessedly unchanged. We used to amaze foreign visitors by walking them from Notting Hill to Westminster through a succession of parks; London is really wonderfully full of green.

In other ways Notting Hill has changed utterly. The war brought some bombing, and also ended for ever the 'upstairs downstairs' style of the big painted stucco houses. Until they found a new life much later as flats and hotels, there was a decrepit run-down feel. It had always been a bit sinister north of Westbourne Grove—gentrification is now moving further and further north, but before the war that whole district was an unexplored mystery. Portobello Road was totally forbidden, reputedly the haunt of thieves. Now Notting Hill is fashionable, no longer a centre of Anglo-Jewry, and unrecognizably trendy with its smart restaurants and company lets—all this came later, a steep revival after an equally steep decline. A murder shortly after the war in the street next to Pembridge Place led to a newspaper article talking of 'a rowdy and ill-lit district'. Many houses were empty, and the stucco had become shabby. It was time to move out.

I was sorry to move. Our house, come to think of it, was appallingly planned, with a huge semi-basement kitchen which had a coke-fired boiler, a large oven, a dresser—and no water. There was the scullery across a passage with a sink and lots of cupboards. The dining room was directly above the kitchen, but the food lift was at the other end of the house, so everything had to be taken and fetched the longest possible distance. And the stairs down to the semi-basement were bare rough wood with a rope for a banister. Still, I'm sure it could all have been modernized—no doubt it has been—and I never really liked the suburban comfort of Hocroft Road, at the very edge of Hampstead. My father liked the garden there though, and was happy growing vegetables and supplying all his family with far more beans than we could eat. By the time we moved, Rosalind was in Paris, so she never felt that Hocroft Road was her home. Our house in Pembridge Place had only a small walled garden, not improved by the concrete air raid shelter at the far end. By the time I remember it, David and Rosalind, as the eldest, had their own rooms, but Colin and Roland shared, and I shared with Evi. In fact Colin and Roland still shared when they were in the navy in the war. Once when they were both on leave together and we had all gone out, a burglar came in and, as my mother heard to her shame at the subsequent trial, the total chaos in their room made the burglar leave in panic, thinking someone else must be on the job already. That says something about the virtue of untidiness.

Nannie's room was always a friendly haven. When David was a baby, my mother, who had seen her own baby brother die from what she thought might have been incompetent management, was nervous at any sign of minor problems. So Nannie came to give her help and confidence, and gave it to us all for many years. She lived with us until the outbreak of war, when she moved back to her family cottage in Church Stretton,

FIG. I. Our parents, Ellis and Muriel Franklin, about 1960 (photo Peter Fisher).

FIG. 2. Nannie (Ada Griffiths), at our wedding, 1958 (photo Peter Fisher).

Shropshire. We often visited her for holidays, and I remember that Rosalind and I were both with her there listening to the radio when the story broke about the atomic bomb on Hiroshima, and Rosalind tried to explain to us what it all meant.

My father was a merchant banker, a profession that has changed in its scope and its overtones as much as Notting Hill itself. He made a comfortable, but by no means wildly profitable, living; he did not find it unduly stressful, and work finished at around five. We were brought up never to talk about money—which presumably means we always had enough. Rosalind once told me that she was acutely embarrassed when, as a small child at school, she had to recite Stevenson's poem 'The Lamplighter', which has the line 'my papa's a banker and as rich as he can be'. He wasn't; our grandparents, with a large country house, acres of garden, and what seemed an army of servants and gardeners, must have been rich, but our banker papa could only be described as conventionally well off. In her first term at Cambridge, anxious to join a National Union of Students trip, Rosalind explained to our parents that with her savings and her birthday money and £5 from Grandpa for getting into Cambridge, she really could afford it. We did have a good-size Victorian house—though my brothers had to share a bedroom—we went to private schools, we rented a big house for a month by the sea in the summer, and we had servants until the war changed all that. But our party dresses and best coats were presents from our grandparents, and our various musical instruments were bought (by all of us except Rosalind, who didn't want one) with money left to us by them. All this made Rosalind, though generous to others, almost mean to herself. It helped her to tolerate living on a ridiculously small salary in Paris (when anyway English money could not be exported), or to make a point of aiming for the cheapest possible holiday accommodation; she positively liked travelling with very little money because, as she told Anne Sayre, 'then you need your wits'. Joining me on her last holiday in Italy in 1957, weakness from her illness made her consent to come in a car, but she wrote sadly that 'travelling around in a little tin box isolates one from the people and the atmosphere of the place in a way that I have never experienced before. I found myself eyeing with envy all rucksacks and tents.' She had to be persuaded to use inherited money to buy a car herself or to furnish her flat. The car, which has been cited as a sign of affluence, was in fact the cheapest new car on the market, a baby Austin; she had no desire to spend time tinkering with an ancient one.

It was only the chances of the First World War that had sent my father to the City at all. He had planned to study physics at Oxford, which would have been a bond between him and Rosalind, but army service, and marriage in 1917, led him to accept work which he had earlier wanted to avoid (although he became extremely good at it), joining his father in the family-based bank of A. Keyser & Co. Physics remained a strong interest in his life—he taught a physics class at the Working Men's College where a lab was later named in his honour. This was the college that had been founded in 1854 by Frederick Denison Maurice and his fellow Christian Socialists to provide education and, as far as possible, a college atmosphere, for those who had not been able to have access to any college; teachers were all unpaid. In fact the more interesting part of my father's life lay in unpaid work outside banking hours, with the Working Men's College (where he became bursar and vice-principal), and with the Jewish Board of Guardians (where he became treasurer and chairman of the executive committee). But Rosalind was not sympathetic to any of this. Merchant banking was then an aggressively male occupation, with Keyser's not even employing women as typists until 1953; she resented the exclusion of women from the Working Men's College, where they were then only allowed the 'vicar's wife' activities of helping in the background or making sandwiches for sports days; and she was indifferent to Jewish charities until the rise of Hitler changed everything.

This raises the question of Rosalind's Jewishness and whether she ever felt herself to be the victim of anti-Semitism. The simple answer to the second part is 'no'. A Newnham friend reported later that a colleague once said to her 'I don't know what you see in Ros—you know she is a Jew don't you'; she hadn't known, but it made no difference to her and Rosalind never knew of the remark, though perhaps it was symbolic of a feeling some may have had behind her back. There was no restriction on the number of Jews at her schools or her university; many of her closest friends were not Jews, but it happened that many of her closest scientific colleagues were—Vittorio Luzzati in Paris, Aaron Klug at Birkbeck; a high proportion of scientists are. Vittorio Luzzati and Rosalind had known each other for some time before they each discovered that the other was Jewish. Rosalind's Jewishness is not easy to define. She was not in any way religious, but Judaism is broader than that, and she always thought of herself as a Jew. This sense of belonging would probably have made her worry about the idea of marrying a non-Jew if the problem arose, but I don't think it ever did. Roughly half of Rosalind's cousins and second cousins, though none of her siblings, did in fact marry non-Jews. None of us were ever aware of anti-Semitism in our own lives, never felt we were outsiders with any obstacles to our jobs or careers. Rosalind once wrote that she felt more European than English, and it may well have been her Jewishness that helped to produce the international outlook that made her feel happily at home on the continent.

In some ways, even if not sympathetic to many of his activities, Rosalind was very like my father. They both had the same basic strong sense of morality, though it showed itself in different ways. For my father it showed in 'good works', and in his clear business ethics. For Rosalind it showed in an outspoken honesty and an extreme sense of justice that could at times make things difficult for her.

Good works were also a feature of my mother's life. She was a Waley, daughter of a rather unsuccessful barrister, granddaughter of a notably distinguished one. Arthur Waley, the orientalist, was her cousin. To her lasting regret, she had been given only the conventional Edwardian female middle-class smatter schooling (while her brother went to university) and she was determined not to do the same to us. She looked after us with the help of our nanny, she ran the household with the help of maids and a cook, and so she had time, and a genuine desire, to do what she could for anyone in need—unmarried mothers, the unemployed, refugees, the elderly. She was a stronger character than many realized , becoming chairman of any committee she was involved in. Submitting to my father's views if she disagreed on minor points, she had the strength (as we will see in Rosalind's case in 1939) to argue forcefully when she felt it mattered.

Arguments, with no ill-feeling on either side, were very much a family feature. My paternal grandparents, who were Liberals, had six children, three of whom became active for women's suffrage, including two who stood for Parliament as Socialists. My father's sister, Helen, known to the family as Mamie, was one of these, and she and my father were the best of friends, although their political views were outspoken and very different. His brother Hugh was more of a problem; his politics were more than my father could take, for he even went to prison and suffered force-feeding for his suffrage activities—stone-throwing, attempts to set fire to a train, and to horsewhip Winston Churchill. But there was still family affection, and Rosalind's second name, 'Elsie', was given in memory of Hugh's first wife, who had died in the flu epidemic after the First World War.

There were not such extreme views in my generation, but there was still a strong tradition of independent thought. So Rosalind found it natural to argue at home about her views and her ambitions, and she enjoyed arguments about work with scientific colleagues. We find her writing happily from Jerusalem in 1953 that she had 'talked and argued endlessly'. Silence or failure to communicate bothered her, but energetic discussions she always found stimulating.

CHAPTER 2

Childhood and Early Schooling

The capacity for intelligent listening and comment appeared early. My mother recorded that Rosalind, still a child, refusing to believe what she was told about the existence of God, had asked 'Well, anyhow, how do you know He isn't a She?' This was simply logic, not early feminism. There is logic too in a letter written when she was about ten, defending herself against some failure to respond as expected: 'I *do* have a letter by my side when I write, but I did not answer that question because I could not decide the answer.' There was imagination, as well as logic, in this intelligent child—like many small children she had imaginary playmates, hers being called, no one knew why, Tinker and Duster.

She was in some ways precocious. Very early on, she had shown herself to be remarkably articulate, teasing David verbally when she was only two years old. Much has been made of a letter from Mamie[1] describing Rosalind as 'alarmingly clever' at the age of six—'alarming', it has been suggested, because she was female and it was worrying that she might be cleverer than her brothers;

FIG. 3. Rosalind, aged about fifteen months.

but it was nothing of the sort—my parents were delighted to have intelligent children of either sex, sent us all to academic schools, expected us all to go to university, and were well used to intelligent women in the family. My paternal grandmother, with a diploma in social science from Bedford College, was highly intelligent, and philanthropically active. Mamie herself, who was on holiday with our family in Cornwall when she wrote that letter, was living at that time in Mandate Palestine, the wife of Norman Bentwich, the Attorney General; later she was to become chairman of the then London County Council. It was simply a sympathetic remark made by an understanding childless aunt—just such a remark as Rosalind herself might have made in her turn.

In fact our childless aunts, Alice and Mamie, seem to feature quite often in Rosalind's own childhood, taking her out and, later, having her to stay for holidays. I remember that Alice, my father's elder sister, used to give each older child £1 at Christmas, and 10 shillings (50p) for the younger ones. I think this stopped at the beginning of the war, for I never progressed to £1.

Alice and Mamie's work, like their mother's, was unpaid. The new generation was different, and it took some time for my father to get used to the idea of women with careers in paid jobs. The Sex Disqualification Removal Bill had been passed only in 1919; women had had the vote on the same terms as men only since 1928. There had been women doctors earlier, thanks largely to the determination of Elizabeth Garrett Anderson, even if the only place in England for their clinical training was still the Royal Free Hospital. But professional women scientists? It is worth noting that although there were women scientists, there were very few by then in any prominent position. There were none in the Royal Society until 1945,

FIG. 4. Chartridge: Rosalind aged about four (with hat) with our cousins Ursula and Irene. Grandma is sitting holding Colin (photo courtesy Norman Franklin).

and no English woman won a Nobel Prize for science before Dorothy Hodgkin in 1964.

My grandparents' country house, at Chartridge in Buckinghamshire, played an important part in our childhood. To quote an early letter of Rosalind's:

> We are having great fun here. We went to the farm in the morning and headoverheeled all the way down the bank... We have got a jar of frog's spawn and a newt which we caught in the bulrush pond. We do not no what to feed him on, Monica [our oldest cousin] sais worms and raw meat but he does not eat much.

Rosalind's spelling was always doubtful. This must have been from a holiday without parents, but we would generally go there on alternate weekends with them, and for a longer time in the summer holidays, often at the same time as our cousins. My first memory of Rosalind is of an occasion in Chartridge when, aged about four, I was drawing in the garden. She tried to explain to me that if you look at the sky it appears to come down to meet the ground; I didn't believe her and went on leaving a proper gap in my drawing, but her explanation, as always when dealing with someone who had a genuine difficulty in understanding, was careful and patient.

Chartridge had everything we could possibly want—tennis court, croquet lawn, woods, ponds, mushrooms, a small farm and a dairy, lots of chickens, a walled vegetable garden, hothouses with forbidden peaches and grapes, a Dark Room where the older children could experiment with photography, and good countryside for long walks. There were clearly understood limits—we never dreamt of penetrating to our grandparents' bedroom, or indeed to their studies without invitation—but apart from those limits we had complete freedom. Sadly, the death of my grandparents and the start of the war ended it all. The house was sold, and although my uncle Cecil and his wife kept part of the garden and a cottage for a while, the magic had gone.

My grandfather, who had had TB, had long been neurotic about his health. To escape the rigours of an English winter, he had developed the habit of renting a villa for some months in Mentone, and occasionally taking his oldest grandchildren for their first experience of France. Rosalind first qualified at Christmas 1929.

My mother's parents did not have the same importance in our lives. They lived, as it happened, in Palace Gardens Terrace, within walking distance of Pembridge Place, so we visited regularly but there was no question of going to stay for a weekend. My grandfather died in 1935, while my grandmother lived on for another nine years as an invalid, semi-paralysed and deaf, though mentally alert and reading to the end.

When she was nine Rosalind left Norland Place, the private day school nearby, and was sent for a couple of years to Lindores, a boarding school in Sussex, 'a cheerful country house in a large garden a short distance from the sea', according to my mother. This was in the (perhaps mistaken) belief that a school by the sea would be good for what was seen as her 'delicate health'—maybe she had had more than her share of

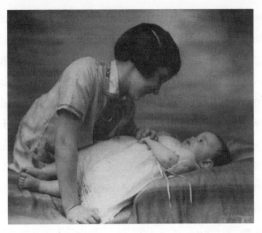

FIG. 5. Rosalind, aged nine, with me.

normal childhood illnesses. I of course have no memory of Rosalind's views at this time, but I know that in retrospect she resented the exile, saying it was totally unnecessary. I have a school prospectus, with its hope 'that when the time comes for a pupil to leave school she may be equipped to occupy with grace and dignity her position in life as a gentle-woman', and its belief that organized games would encour-age 'love of justice, power of obedience, self-control, prompt decision, and a cheerful recognition of defeat'—I'm not sure that all this was absorbed by Rosalind. At any rate I welcome her childish letters home, with gradually improving hand-writing, even if they are mostly about the minutiae of board-ing school life—games, marks, weather, making presents for birthdays and Christmas, the number of days to the holidays, or other standard minor worries. 'I like boarding school on the whole,' she wrote to Roland (then aged about four), 'although we do have jam pudding sometimes.' She was naturally anxious for news from home: the number of mice the cat had caught, my progress in growing and crawling— 'When does David break up? I hope the newts are quite well. Does Colin like Devon House? I am putting my letter for Roland in here, with a used stamp on it. Please give it him on his birthday as if it has come from the post.' And 'I went to bed early in punishment with Janet yesterday and for an hour we were rushing up and down stairs looking for somebody to give us our hot water, and also to wipe up a whole jug of cold water which we spilt and in the end we did not get into bed till the rest came up, after mopping the mess up with sponges and flannels.' These letters were written, as her letters always

FIG. 6. Lindores School (from school prospectus, about 1940).

were, with the fluency of speech, so that Rosalind's character comes through. They generally seem cheerful enough, but there is one defiant answer to my mother: 'You say we come to school partly to learn to control our exitement, well everybody has been exited about coming home, since half-term, and now we are all terribly exited about it.'

A reminder of the primitive state of the wireless in 1930 comes in one letter when she says that she and her fellow piano pupils were allowed to stay up to hear their teacher broadcasting at 9 o'clock one evening: 'We waited till about 9.45 but still they could not get anything but noises, so we had to go up to bed.'

Considering her later indifference, she writes surprisingly often about music. But the early stages of piano playing can be achieved quite well and satisfyingly by anyone with a reasonable sense of rhythm, manual dexterity, and good coordination (which she certainly had), and without much musical ability (which she unfortunately hadn't). So she dutifully practised and took her early exams—though she had problems with singing, reporting that she 'went all the way up and down the scale with only three mistakes'. Another extra-curricular duty, carried out without obvious protest, was responding to Hebrew exercises sent to her, to be done while her schoolfellows went to church. She did not seem bothered by being 'odd one out'.

Other comments give something more of her character and the general atmosphere of the school, and show her constantly busy reading, playing games, sewing, swimming, making things, often for her family or for Nannie (who was virtually part of the family): 'I have finished Jen's beret, but I think it will be too small. One row has all gone brown, I think it must have been off the needles,' she wrote. And again:

> I shall want a new bathing dress for the holidays, a big peace has come out of one shoulder, and I have sewn it up without it, so it is very tight, and a little piece out of the other side, with the button on, which I lost, and the only one I could find was a tiny one which is always slipping undone, as I sewed it on the wrong side, and is fraying all round the edges.

She was often top in arithmetic; history was a bit woollier—'We have finished Henry VIII but have not started whoever comes next'. Two passing thoughts to end these quotations—'I think I'll become an editor [of the school magazine?—there's no further explanation in the letter], and then I might get a shilling a week', and 'I won't have to rest or go to bed at seven in the holidays now, will I? I never go to bed till quarter to eight now, and never rest.' Resting, as Gwen Raverat wrote, is far too exhausting for children.[2]

Literature was studied in a way unimaginable for ten-year-olds today—Shakespeare plays, Elizabethan poetry, the Golden Treasury. 'I have read the hole of a large edition of "Kidnapped" this term. We are reading "Hiawatha" in literature this term, and "Gulliver's Travels" in reading.'

Another good feature of that school, much appreciated by Rosalind, was the occasional visiting lecturer. There was, she reported, one on 'the different ways of a river beggining'; one on 'see stories' (ships, explorers, the 1914 War); one on Palestine (including her great uncle Herbert Samuel, then High Commissioner); others on 'self defence of animals', 'travelling across Canada', 'Normandy'—'Where was Joan of Arc burned, he said Rouen but I thought it was Orleans'.

A bad feature was the spying on all letters apart from letters home (so Rosalind tended to enclose others to be forwarded):

> I wrote to Dadsnana [my father's old nanny] last Sunday, but I left the envelope open, and last Monday I had to write out the envelope exactly ten times because it was not neet enough, and yesterday I had to write the inside out twice…I am just going to write Dadsnana's letter for the fifth time.

One letter mentions 'David's solution', so these two, aged around ten and eleven, clearly enjoyed puzzles and scoring off each other. Puzzles were always a pleasure; Rosalind enjoyed challenging my father with word problems. Once, David showed off by writing her a letter in French, which she had to get a teacher to translate.

But the best and most memorable times of childhood are not schooldays but holidays, and our parents organized these with imaginative enthusiasm. We would rent a large house and spend at least a month by the sea, generally in Cornwall or Wales, often joined by various friends and relations. We took pride in choosing places that were, in those

FIG. 7. Family holiday at St David's, 1930.

FIG. 8. All five of us, in the brief time when Rosalind (aged about eleven) was taller than our oldest brother David.

days, fairly remote and unspoilt—I remember the family's horror when a car park, and all it implied, first appeared on the St David's cliffs.

My parents had a great belief in the virtues of sea air, but after a couple of years they reckoned that a country school in Bexhill had done its job, and that Rosalind was now ready for the rigours of St Paul's.

CHAPTER 3

Early Education of a Scientist

St Paul's Girls' School had been founded in 1904, only twenty-seven years before Rosalind arrived. The High Mistress was only the second in the life of the school—and was still in command throughout my time there, ten years later. It was, and is, in a green part of Hammersmith, with buildings in orange brick with white stone, designed by Gerald Horsley, a pupil of Norman Shaw and one of the founders of the Art Workers Guild.

In the middle-class conventional way, my brothers were all sent in turn to a boarding public school—to Oundle because my father, who himself had been to the Jewish house at Clifton, did not approve of religious segregation. Rosalind had had enough of boarding, and anyway girls were a different problem and there does not seem to have been any question of sending her away again. So St Paul's Girls' School was an obvious choice. Academic standards were high, the curriculum was wide, Mamie had been there in its very early days, several cousins were happily established there already, and, though too far away to walk, it was on a direct bus route

FIG. 9. St Paul's Girls' School (photo taken 1922, sent by Howard Bailes, St Paul's librarian).

from Pembridge Place—no one would think of being driven to school in those days. I think our first car—called Methuselah because of its great age—was bought in about the year Rosalind started at St Paul's, and it was used only for holidays and for journeys to the Working Men's College playing fields at Edgware, or to Chartridge. It was kept in the Lex Garage at the end of the road (now a row of unconvincing pastiche white houses), for the original Pembridge Place houses, built around 1850, had no space for cars and there was then no street parking.

Rosalind was eleven when she went to St Paul's. Early traces of a careful and excited scientist had already appeared. Colin has written how:

Developing and printing photographs at home, with my mother, was a discovery which thrilled her in childhood, swilling the sensitised paper in a tray of water where stuff called 'hypo' as I recall, in crystal form looking like coffee sugar, was dissolved; watching the image appear, removing it at the right moment of development.[1] I remember her exclamation which pleased my mother, 'It makes me feel all squidgy inside'.

Indeed, many traits of her character were already clear—her intelligence, her skill with her hands, her perfectionism, her logical mind, her outspoken honesty. I still have some of her meticulous school projects—a specially impressive one, done enthusiastically with her friend Jean Kerslake, was on 'Florence, the home of Art'; 'in choice of material & illustration in mounting and drawing, excellent work,' wrote their appreciative teacher. Rosalind had obviously enjoyed becoming thoroughly involved, had been to the National Gallery, borrowed 'a lovely book about Botticelli' from a great-aunt, more books from grandparents. This scholarly approach was there all her life, from the time when, as my mother wrote, 'as a tiny child she could never accept a belief or statement for which no reason or proof could be produced'. Jean's parents later told her that, as she wrote to my brother Colin, 'Rosalind won me my scholarship to Newnham by teaching me how to work'. In Jean's memory:

> Our academic enthusiasm extended to all subjects, and we devoted much time to testing each other's homework and comparing notes…We were equally enthusiastic about gym and games…In the society and politics of the form, we were not

among the leading group, from which form and games captains were chosen. However we were accepted by the group, and invited to their houses. In order to be acceptable, one had to be mentally, physically and emotionally tough; weakness of any kind was not tolerated...We both moved from the guide companies we had originally joined to the school company. We became patrol leaders, enjoyed the annual camp and acquired various proficiency badges.[2]

Another school friend, Anne Crawford (later, as Anne Piper, the headmistress of a big London comprehensive school), in a tribute in 1998, wrote that Rosalind always beat her as top of the class. She worked hard, in that competitive school. Annually, she won prizes. Early ones, chosen by the school, were volumes

FIG. 10. Form hockey team at St Paul's. Rosalind is in the back row, on the extreme right.

of poetry, followed by a life of John Colet, the founder of St Paul's School. Later, her own tastes were allowed to appear, and she chose Eddington's *New Pathways in Science* and Trevelyan's *British History in the Nineteenth Century*. I have them all, in their handsome scarlet leather binding, together with my father's prizes from Clifton which, bound in dark blue leather, were always sternly scientific, ending with an apparently unread collection of Darwin.

Rosalind had a good ear for languages, learning some German, as scientists did in those days, because important scientific papers were often in German, and later becoming totally fluent in colloquial French; on holiday in Italy in 1949 she reckoned that she could follow the conversations though she couldn't take part. But an ear for music is a different matter, and here she admitted defeat. Jean felt that this gap meant that Rosalind missed a lot, as music was a fine feature of the school. Poor Gustav Holst, the school music director, asked my mother to come to see him, hoping Rosalind might have some problem with her hearing or her tonsils—I'm afraid Rosalind spoilt his optimistic belief that everyone had music in them.

Later Rosalind tried to analyse her feelings about music. It gave so much pleasure to her school friends and to the rest of our family, and she wanted to understand why it gave none to her. She decided, in a letter from Paris in about 1949, after describing her happiness at a wonderful performance of *Swan Lake*, that she didn't enjoy listening to opera or any singing, but did enjoy classical ballet and could get something out of concerts in a good concert hall—though perhaps no more than she might get from hearing music on a wireless.

Since St Paul's is normally a day school, there are generally no letters from her time there, but dutiful letters to her grandfather have survived, and she did stay in the school's boarding house on two brief occasions when my parents were away. I find it touching to see how she wrote to them about everything that they might find interesting, from her own activities to news from her visits home at weekends—reports of the garden, of mending the hose with sticking plaster and Seccotine, or of my progress in blowing bubbles. A planned expedition to a 'folk-dancing thing' fell through without many regrets, but she was upset at the thought of missing the Royal Tournament, though when she was older she would have hated such a display; she did go in the end, and at fourteen she found it 'marvellous', especially 'the musical ride and the motor-cycle and horse thing'. At sixteen, still thoroughly royalist, she was thanking Grandpa for 'a really wonderful day' watching the coronation procession for George VI.

One letter, written when she was about thirteen, does give a clue to her future interests: 'We spent the whole arithmetic lesson to-day with a lovely discussion about gravity and all that sort of stuff.' Another, after indignation at her essay mark, gives doubts about her own ability in exams, doubts which were to reappear throughout her time at school and Cambridge:

I only got B to B+ for that essay, which is very bad (I told you she was an old pig). I am not quite sure if I want to go in for senior schol., but may I? it has several advantages, and there is no danger whatsoever of my getting it. First advantage, it comes the same week as school exams, which you miss if you go in for it, I should rather like to see what the papers are like, and you get a lot of extra baths and things, and I don't have to stodge through The Rivals, School for Scandal, and The Critic, which are too dreary for anything, and which we will have to know for the school English exam. We are having gorgeous geography lessons, learning to weather forecast.

She did get the scholarship of course. Grandpa was delighted and gave her £5, which she told him she would spend on books, the first instalment being *A History of Exploration* by Percy Sykes, and *Everyman's Encyclopedia*, 'which I shall find tremendously useful as before we had no encyclopedia larger than the little Routledge one'. I find it surprising that we were so badly equipped.

Exam worries became worse. When I first remember her, words like 'homework' and 'matric'[3] seemed to dominate her life. My two elder brothers were away at school by this time, so I can't compare her approach to work with theirs, but certainly I remember her going off to her room to study, and feeling that what she did was important, not to be disturbed. I admired her but was worried, sure (quite rightly) that I would never work as hard as that. She also, as Jean has written, entered enthusiastically into other sides of school life, including, I particularly remember because I enjoyed being allowed to go along, sales in aid of the school charity in Stepney.

Tennis and hockey were both prominent in Rosalind's school life, and she was not forbidden, as the previous Franklin generation had been, to be in school teams and play in matches on Saturdays (the Jewish Sabbath); Mamie remembered this prohibition as 'the only real disadvantage I have felt in being Jewish'.

Rosalind's school certificate, in spite of the usual exam nerves, brought her six distinctions, an easy overkill for matric. For she was able at all subjects, and particularly interested in history, though she never doubted that specialization meant science. And it was to be physical sciences and maths, not biology or botany which were mainly for those wanting to be doctors. You might expect someone so talented, and so keen to succeed, in sport as well as academically, to be something of a favourite among the teachers, but in fact they found Rosalind reserved and difficult. She had her close friends at school, particularly Jean and Anne, and they remained friends all her life, but she did not easily open up to others. Somehow her teachers must have fallen into the category of those she failed to communicate with, not those with whom she could enjoy discussions or arguments.

In 1935, when she was still at school, she and David had joined my parents on a holiday in Norway. There is a letter to Grandpa, full of excitement at her first mountains:

> We went with a guide, up on top of the glacier, 4,600 feet up. It was a marvellous walk. We saw over the top of the mountains all round, and a long way down the fjord. The glacier itself was the finest thing I have ever seen.

Her greatest aesthetic pleasure was always in scenery, in cliffs and coasts, and above all in mountain scenery. In this she was very like my father.

The excursion to Norway was the best of all family holidays, to be repeated in 1937 and, after her first year at Cambridge, 1939. In 1937 both her younger brothers were there too; Colin

FIG. 11. Rosalind in the mountains on a family holiday in Norway, 1937 or 1939.

remembers that holiday, and remembers Rosalind's 'delight in watching wave-formations from the ship's bows as we crossed to Bergen, all in accordance with something to do with wavelengths she had learnt at school'. In 1939 we all went, a rash journey undertaken because I had never been abroad, and my father rightly felt that I might not have the opportunity again for a long time. While we were in Fjaerland we heard that Russia

had signed a pact with Germany, so, against all childish pro-
tests, we were rushed home, learning while we were on the way
that war had been declared.

Cambridge, it was assumed, was the best place for science
and, after consultation with friends and relatives, Rosalind
decided Newnham was more desirable than Girton (the only
two women's colleges in the University), and that by 1938 she
was very ready to move. From the school's point of view, it was
a year early—they would have liked her to stay on and probably
get a scholarship. She had the usual worries about exams and
was of course unnecessarily worried by her interviews: 'My
feelings about the physics are mixed. By a huge stroke of luck
both things were in the half of the syllabus that I have done, but
I made a pretty bad mess of one of them.' In the end Rosalind,
with the highest marks in the chemistry paper, got a school
leaving exhibition and a prize. Six months later she would be at
Newnham, and writing home for all the things she had forgotten or found she needed—matric form, walking shoes, eider-
down, and her picture of Paris, apart from all the equipment
she intended to buy at Woolworths for her room.

Exams behind her, Rosalind's summer term at St Paul's was
more relaxing and full of variety—though of rather a serious
kind. She wrote a long letter to Grandpa at Chartridge, describing a visit to Hammersmith Borough Council, and then:

> Aunt Mamie is taking Irene [Rosalind's cousin] and me to an air
> raid demonstration in Kensington, and before that I am going
> with a friend to the Chelsea Flower Show. Yesterday evening we
> had a debate at school, the motion being that 'a return to secret
> diplomacy would further the cause of world peace'. So altogether,

I have got rather a full week. I am doing very little work, and am altogether rather enjoying this term.

St Paul's now honours her with the 'Rosalind Franklin Technology Centre', and cites her with pride as a distinguished Old Girl. So, besides good exam results, what had St Paul's given her? She had learnt how to work hard, she knew where her interests lay, and she had found permanent friends—'I like my St Paul's friends so much better than any of the English girls I have met since,' she wrote to my parents from Paris in 1950. She had become more sure of herself, and she had begun her training as a scientist.

She had six weeks of French culture in an establishment for foreigners just outside Paris in the summer of 1938, learning French and having some experience of independent life before the rigours of Cambridge—the only one of us to have this early and brief version of a student's 'gap year'. Since she was away from home, we have a burst of letters from this visit, not as endearing as her childish ones, but still spontaneous as if she were talking, and full of details of her life, showing how she was making the most of a busy programme. She was, she explained, far too busy to conform to the family habit of keeping a diary of her travels, but she seems to have used her letters to give a full account of everything she did. She went by air, 'a delightful way of travelling,' she told our parents, 'you must try next time you go anywhere'. In spite of worries that the place might turn out to be, of all horrors, a sort of finishing school for young ladies, the visit was a success:

This is a big house, quite near the river, and I have got a nice room with two big windows. Madame is very nice, but not at all what I expected.

Life was busy:

> When we go to Paris we go soon after lunch and do not get back till supper time, and after supper we talk (French, which I don't want to miss), or else go for a walk by the river. The mornings are mainly occupied by French lessons and coup [dressmaking]. In fact, I find when I want to do any work 6.30 a.m. is the only time.

They made good use of the river, bathing and boating in their leisure time, with freedom to explore the country around even if that was regarded as slightly eccentric. Her journey with an old school friend to Chantilly, involving a walk of twenty kilometres or so, was hardly believed:

> If anybody in France walks more than about four kilometres they are considered a little bit mad. When I said I had walked twenty they said it was an impossibility! I had not realised it was as bad as that as the family here are better than most French people in that way.

Telephoning was complicated in those days and definitely to be discouraged:

> When you telephoned before I came Guite [one of the host family] had got your wire and arranged with the exchange that when there was a call from London for her number which no longer exists they should put it through to the cafe round the corner, where she waited for it.

There was plenty of sightseeing—Notre Dame, the Arc de Triomphe, the Louvre, Napoleon's house, Victor Hugo's house, the Château de Vincennes, Versailles, endless museums (and endless disappointments when they were found to be shut), an exciting visit to the astronomy and chemistry sections of the Palais de la Découverte, films, plays, churches, a mosque, and the festivities to welcome King George—in those days she didn't have the horror of crowds that bothered her when victory was celebrated in England in 1945. The king's visit came just after the processions and fireworks for 14 July, so all Paris was decorated and in holiday mood. Rosalind, in a letter of 15 July, gives an unexpected picture of French politics at the time.

> Driving through Paris we saw not one communist flag—they say last year there were just as many red flags as tricolours. I do not know quite the significance of that, as there is still a large communist party, but things here are now much more settled than this time last year. There were less restrictions this year, and it all went off very peacefully. Last year they were forbidden to sing the Marseillaise for fear of provoking a row.

The next week, she had a happy time seeing the arrival of the king, and the river procession for him.

Rosalind enjoyed the dressmaking lessons: 'I spent 100 francs today on the stuff for my dress, which I now find looks enough for a dress and several carpets'; she acquired the skill which she put to good use in the 'make-do-and-mend' wartime days. Above all though, she was learning French, having formal lessons, and trying to talk French with her fellow students, even when the tutors were not around. Her fluency still seemed to her frustratingly inadequate. She told my father that he was far too optimistic when he talked of 'perfecting' her French: 'I cannot argue with a French person, though I often want to, because as soon as I begin they talk so fast that I cannot understand'—the penalty of having a good accent and correct grammar. 'I think I shall know enough to read easily, which is what I most want, though I should like to be able to talk too.' Conscientiously, she wondered whether to concentrate on conversation, reading, or listening. She arranged to have two extra lessons a week.

Studiously, she wrote home for 'some of my own money, to spend on French books for myself. I intend to read some on the holidays to try and fix a little French in my mind.' She also asked for money for her ticket home, at prices ranging from 335 francs for Boulogne to Folkestone third class, to 495 francs for Calais to Dover second class; she was sent a 495-franc ticket.

> I have so much that I want to do in these last few days that I don't know where to begin or which to choose…I hope to have a last day in Paris, possibly the Louvre and Palais de la Decouverte again…I shall be very sorry to leave here.

The love of France and all things French stayed with her for the rest of her life.

CHAPTER 4

A Science Student
in Wartime Cambridge

B y 1938 Newnham College had been established nearly seventy years. It had even finer 'Queen Anne' style buildings than St Paul's School; the architect was Basil Champneys. The days of chaperones and compulsory hats were over, but women, limited to a total of 550 between the two Cambridge women's colleges, Newnham and Girton, were not yet fully part of the University. Some pre-war customs now seem as distant as costume dramas—freshers of each Hall, to Rosalind's dismay, had to provide an entertainment for the end of term; protesting she objected to acting, she was given a walk-on part in a crowd scene. Even worse, and hardly believably, two from each Hall— Newnham was divided into four Halls—had to go each Monday evening and dance with the maids. It was difficult to conform to such things, but they were minor drawbacks in the exciting move.

There is a myth, which doesn't seem to disappear although Brenda Maddox has rightly attacked it, that my father didn't approve of girls studying science or going to university.

FIG. 12. Newnham College (photo Alan Davidson).

The truth is that my father, whose own scientific interests had been frustrated, was proud of Rosalind going to Cambridge in 1938. The trouble came the following year, with the outbreak of the Second World War, when my father felt that Rosalind should do something directly connected with the war. His sisters, in the previous crisis, had joined the Land Army, and Rosalind had a hard time persuading him that that would be entirely wrong for her, and that she might be more useful if she completed her chemistry degree. All my brothers had their careers interrupted or changed by the war (as my father's had been)— David left Oxford in 1939, after only two years, to join the army, and never felt able to settle back there again although he tried briefly when he was demobilized; Colin was in the navy from 1942, eventually going to Oxford at the age of twenty-three; Roland joined the navy as the war ended and, deciding to get married when he was released, never had the Cambridge years that had been planned. As my father saw it, Rosalind was taking an unwarranted soft option. This was the time when my mother, supported by my Aunt Alice, firmly took Rosalind's side, convinced that she was right in wanting to stay at Newnham. Rosalind was, as she herself explained to my father, anxious to do some sort of war work in the vacations, helping my parents with their work for refugees, and was anxious, too, to have some sort of war work using her scientific skills when she graduated—it was then, after all, 1941, and the country was still in crisis. By the time the war was over, the direction of Rosalind's life was clear.

Rosalind was the only scientist among the five of us, but there were others in the extended family and could well have been more. My father's physics had been aborted, his brother Hugh had gone to Cambridge to study engineering, but had abandoned it when suffrage activities took over his life. (One relic of his training was an effort to design and build an aeroplane in a field at Chartridge—it nearly flew.) Then there were various scientific cousins—two first cousins who read chemistry, and several second cousins, including one who became a professor of chemistry at the Weizmann Institute in Israel. My Chartridge grandfather, whose main hobby was concern for the Jews of Eastern Europe, was interested in science in a Victorian amateur way, having an elegant microscope, and using a lathe (rather like Prince Bolkonsky in *War and Peace*). We inherited the lathe, installing it in a room my parents had converted into a workshop for us, hoping my brothers would make wonderful things; it was mainly Rosalind who used that workshop.

When she went to Newnham she was just eighteen, younger than most and in many ways young for her age. In her first term she dutifully went home for the Working Men's College Founders' Night—not the sort of thing she would do later. Nor, later, would she bother to keep accounts, as she did after her first bout of shopping, and as our banker father was concerned we should do. Her very full and frequent letters show her gradually maturing from her schoolgirl outlook, when she tended to echo her parents' beliefs (except in religion, which she had already firmly rejected), to her own outspoken left-wing independence. All her life she wrote regularly whenever she was away from home, expecting regular news and views in return—'I only received one letter from each of you in the first two whole weeks,' she complained to my parents in October 1940.

I visited her once, as a nine-year-old, with my parents, in her first year, but I'm afraid all I remember is walking along the Backs and seeing baby ducks.

Gertrude Dyche (née Clark), a contemporary, wrote later:

> I remember her as a very good friend. I myself was described in a report at school as having a 'directness of manner' and looking back I think I valued Ros because I found the same trait in her. She was straightforward, even forthright, and not inclined to be diplomatic. She had very high standards and expected others to have the same.[1]

Gertrude lost touch with Rosalind when she moved to Paris, but there was an unexpected and sad reunion in Rosalind's last days when Gertrude, a physicist at the Royal Marsden Hospital, discovered that Rosalind was there as a patient.

At Newnham Rosalind was (as she remained) serious-minded, and concerned about politics. In her letters she asked for political information, sending her own views, often intending to provoke the discussions and arguments she was used to at home. In Paris she had complained that 'we do not get any newspapers here, as the family disapprove of the politics of all of them'. Would the 'Weekly Times' be any good, she had wondered. In Cambridge she was disappointed at the apparent indifference of many of her fellow students to the crisis in 1938, and worried about the pacifists, and about the communists' blind approval of Russia—there are many caustic comments about a communist cousin's beliefs. Still worried, she wrote in her second year:

> This afternoon three of us attacked a communist for about an hour, while she tried to defend Russia. We were discussing the lack of liberty in Russia, and I mentioned their habit of chopping off the heads of people they don't like. She rose up indignantly and said 'no they don't, they shoot them'.

'Nobody here seems to have taken much notice of what is going on in Germany,' she complained in November 1938, and 'Apart from your letters and The Times, I would still have no idea that anybody objected to Germany's treatment of the Jews'; she did though later find 'a fairly small group of people' who were actively interested. Coming from a concerned and active Jewish family, she had already been involved in the struggle to get Jews out of Germany, recruiting her school friends to help with the administrative problems at the Jewish refugee centre in Woburn House, welcoming Evi, the nine-year-old Austrian girl, into our household, and deflecting her exhibition money to a refugee student.

Was she, as some felt, over-serious, spending her free time only on extra-curricular lectures or college tea or cocoa parties? Her early letters are certainly a bit earnest, worried only that courses of German for science students might clash with chemistry practicals, or concerned, almost as if it were a duty rather than a pleasure, about what to do for exercise. Jean Kerslake, in her 1993 memories of Rosalind, wrote 'I saw little of Rosalind at Cambridge, for she worked extremely hard and I enjoyed a very full social life...I think Rosalind rather disapproved of my flighty behaviour.' 'Sociability' for Rosalind and, according to Gertrude Dyche, for all busy scientists, tended to consist only of 'informal gatherings with friends in college, and university societies'. Within those limits, Rosalind 'was as sociable as any of the other scientists of her year'. Jean, reading classics, probably had more free time as well as an easier temperament. But in her first term Rosalind was planning a skiing holiday in Switzerland and wrote of 'four invitations of various sorts' for the Christmas vacation, so she does not sound too self-contained. The Swiss trip, with David and a party of cousins and friends, was organized by the National Union of Students, who asked for criticisms afterwards—perhaps they were not expecting a response from a student like Rosalind, who of course answered fully.

Rosalind had the usual problems of a beginner in the days before ski lifts made life easier: 'I think I spent one half of the time trying to get up after falling and one quarter slipping down the slope I was trying to climb up.' She took to skiing more thoroughly than to 'after-ski' jollities: 'To-day has been spent by most people recovering from last night. There was a fancy dress dance which lasted till about 4 o'clock, but David and I left soon after 1 and were out skiing before 10 o'clock this morning.' She had gone to the dance as the St Paul's High Mistress, Miss Strudwick, clearly successfully because 'everyone told me I looked like some awful schoolmistress of theirs'.

'As regards skiing,' she wrote rather sadly, 'David and I are the duds of our party. However, we enjoy what we do...I love skiing, and I long to come again and do something more enterprising.' Above all, she longed for France again:

> The chief advantage of France, to my mind, is that it is always so much more exciting to be among people of another country, and much more interesting from the point of view of meeting people—and one meets a lot of people to talk to in youth hostels or other simple accommodation.

But the war checked that, confining her travels to Wales or the Lake District, and she had, I think, only one more skiing holiday, and that was not until 1947 or so, when she went with Roland to Pralognan la Vanoise, in the Savoy Alps. Skiing never gave her the same excitement as climbing, and she never showed great skill at it, but she loved the winter scene.

In her first term at Cambridge, Rosalind joined both the Chemical Society ('a life member as it saves 6s in 3 years') and the Archimedians (the maths club) out of interest, and the Jewish Society out of duty:

> It is no use to me as I have neither Friday evenings nor Saturday mornings free, but I shall have to join as Grandpa has been writing to the professor in charge and I have been asked to lunch there on Sunday.

She did though, without much enthusiasm, go with Rachel Caro (sister of the sculptor) to the Passover evening when it fell in term time in her second year.

Rosalind was overwhelmed by work, and planned to read a lot in the vacation to catch up because, as she soon realized, 'school science was hopelessly inadequate'. 'At present', she wrote, 'I am frightfully bad at practicals, and muddle everything, as I have never done anything but the simplest or most straightforward things before. The elegant science block at school seems to be all show and nothing in it.'

As a relief from work, she enjoyed, as always, walking and cycle rides, exploring the strange fenland countryside—on one of her walks she chanced to meet Hugh and his wife Bunny. 'Simultaneously Uncle Hugh expressed surprise at seeing me and said he did not know I was here, and Aunt Bunny said "There! I told you so, I knew she was here"!'

She played hockey, squash, and tennis, and skated on frozen fens:

Skating continues [she wrote in January 1939]. To-day I went to Lingay Fen, just beyond Granchester, where the all-England championships etc are held. It is specially flooded—a huge expanse of ice, much better than the lake here—a disused gravel pit—but it is much further and costs a shilling. I generally go to the lake by moonlight. It is surprisingly warm, and the ice is empty then.

The following winter, notoriously cold, was also excellent for skating, with ice over six inches thick on the Mill Pond and the river freezing over.

Tennis, at a competent though not too serious level, remained an outlet all Rosalind's life. In London in the early fifties she would play energetically with friends most Sundays at my brother Roland's house in Highgate. Evi remembers her even playing 'with great enthusiasm at the court on Campden Hill in a pause between her hospital stays'. The cycling, hardy even in 1939, sounds alarming in these days of busy roads—'Why were you so surprised about cycling home?' she wrote in her fourth term, 'I want my bike in London and it seems the simplest way of getting it there.' It was a ride of more than fifty miles.

Always ready to fight when she felt hard done by, she wrote to my parents in her second term:

> The complaint about my chemistry lectures was well worth making—I now go to very much better ones, and also, as a necessary change in my timetable to better physics and chemistry labs. I am in the middle of a struggle over maths lectures, but I'm very much afraid I'm on the losing side. The ones I want to go to are on analysis. I have heard from several people who have done the course that they are very interesting and also provide useful short cut methods in physical calculations. The lecturer is very good, though female.

She lost the maths struggle, though, her tutor saying she was 'definitely not in a position to profit by' the best lectures. The other lecturer, she complained, was '*awful*':

> He stands in front of what he is writing and says 'square this' 'take away that' without saying what, and then rubs it off! When we do catch a glimpse of his writing it is generally not more than 1/2 inch high. He also has a maddening habit of walking up and

down the whole length of the room, so that if you are near the gangway, the effect is something like the fragments of conversation one hears when passing someone in the street.

Clearly, even after one term, Rosalind was prepared to protest, to expect the best teaching that could be offered. In a way, it was an expression of her extreme sense of justice; she had come to Cambridge to get the best available teaching, and if she felt she was being deprived of it she was not afraid to say so.

She heard the supervision reports from her second term, and gave her own report on the supervisor:

> There were some rather amusing comments from the mineralogy one, who does not know her subject, and whom I have defeated in arguments on a number of occasions. She said 'she knows her work but does not always keep to the point' and 'she does not seem to take criticism kindly'—both of which mean 'she doesn't agree with me'.

Rosalind may have provoked criticism from her supervisor, but she was still anxious for approval from her parents. 'I gather from David that he has told you of my suggestion of Youth-Hostelling for a week in the Peak District at the beginning of the vac. Do you approve?' she wrote. They did.

Delia Agar, who taught her in her second and third years, was more appreciative: 'She was very anxious to learn and stimulating to supervise,' she wrote, 'always prepared to argue and to answer back. In her third year she was very considerate and helpful to her supervision partner, a girl less academically able than herself. She did work hard—too hard in her final year.'[2]

All too soon, the letters show how war preparations started to invade Newnham life—'I must have my gas mask'; 'they are making a ridiculous fuss about ARP [air-raid precautions]'; 'there is some scheme for digging trenches in the cabbage patch, and rehearsing emptying Newnham into the trenches in five minutes'. Rosalind conformed, but there was a hitch in preparations from 'two pacifists who refuse to send for gas masks or take part in any ARP drill. They have gone to see the Principal about it.' Rehearsals could be farcical:

> One of the dons was standing outside my room waiting to blow a whistle at the given signal. The signal came—and the whistle would not blow! However, as everybody expected it, the intermittent squeaks told them what was meant. We then had to assemble at the garden door, dressed, with coats, blankets and gas masks. All ready for grand exit when Mrs P [the tutor] discovered she had the wrong key, so we could not get out! Long delay while correct key was found.

The only time she reported the Newnham ARP and Red Cross properly in action was when the Newnham rowing eight went under the floodgates in the river, and survived, shaken and cold, with only bruises!

The first year ended in a total exam panic—'a frightful mess' that might mean three years for part I, and no part II:

> I made a disgusting mess of the chemistry, which is most annoying, as it is my best subject, and I had spent practically the whole of last week learning it up. I really knew my notes inside out, but they only enabled me to answer 1 question properly, and we have to do six. Physics, on the other hand, which I had hardly revised

at all because I thought it so hopeless, was not too bad. I think they were all fairly easy papers which I should have done really well. Mineralogy, which I expected to do best in, was a lovely paper but I wasted the first 3/4 hour completely in going about a question the wrong way. The result was a terrific rush and a lot of bad blunders. I think I did best in maths—the one subject which doesn't matter, and which is only 1/2 subject anyway. I have never done anything so badly as yesterday's physics practical—I did 1/2 instead of 2 experiments...It doesn't matter as long as I don't do so badly that I'm not allowed to take Part I next year. With a second I am safe, but with a third, probably not.

Unnecessary panic yet again, because she got a first.

There was a welcome distraction:

There are only two topics of conversation in Newnham at present, 1. exams and 2. skeletons. They have found complete Saxon skeletons about 4 feet down, while digging trenches in the garden. They are really most exciting. The first day they found two—discovered when a man put his pick through one of their skulls. They were all facing east, therefore Christian...All arche-ologists (including the new professor [Dorothy Garrod]) spend their time excavating with desert spoons and tooth brushes.

This is the scene drawn so charmingly by Quentin Blake for his 'Cambridge 800' mural, a panorama of historical events in the University's story to celebrate its 800th anniversary. Rosalind, the only other woman to appear in Blake's mural, had written of the election of Dorothy Garrod as the first woman professor:

apparently it is the custom in Cambridge for a newly-elected professor to be invited to feasts in all the colleges—but never before has a woman been to a feast in a man's college! King's, however, has led the way, in the present case, but has not yet been followed by others. Newnham has a 'college feast' in honour of the occasion.

At Newnham there were, Rosalind wrote, 'some good speeches and terrific enthusiasm'.

A minor exam Rosalind had to take, with amusement rather than worry, was for proficiency in punting so that she would be allowed by the college to go on the river. In a birthday letter to thirteen-year-old Roland she explained that in her last lesson she could only get the boat stuck across the river, and 'now the river is very high, so it will probably be worse'.

FIG. 13. Quentin Blake drawing of Dorothy Garrod digging up bones in Newnham Garden (reproduced by kind permission of Quentin Blake).

In Rosalind's first summer vacation, war started. Unusually, this brought serious division in the family; fortunately, my father was moved by the pressure from my mother and Aunt Alice strongly supporting Rosalind's conviction that she should continue with her science degree. Rosalind, like almost all Cambridge women undergraduates, went back: '90 per cent of Newnham has returned,' she reported triumphantly in October, 'and I do not know of any science person in Newnham or Girton who has not.'

The letters are now full of the minor problems of war. Rosalind took evacuated children for walks, went to a lecture on the tactical use of gas, needed her ration book and her gas mask: 'There are said to be 30,000 evacuees here,' she reported, 'and it can't be particularly safe as there are dozens of aerodromes all round, and government in some of the colleges.' Later the town seemed full of army and air force. Rosalind tried to puzzle out her views on the war so that she could take part in a debate:

> I agree with all you say that is bad in Germany [she wrote home], but the chief point seems to be—were we really threatened with such things ourselves. I don't believe we were, nor do I believe that our motives are entirely unselfish i.e. that we are fighting solely in the cause of small countries. I certainly do believe the war is justified, but it seems to be merely because we couldn't possibly have got out of it—not a very strong argument.

And a little later that same year:

> I hate the way Churchill talks, much as I admire his work. He does all he can to inspire that hate which everyone at the beginning of the war was determined to avoid.

This showed a change from her first year, when she had heard Churchill with the total approval that our parents always felt— 'a brilliant speech, and I thoroughly enjoyed it,' she had written the previous May, when she had been excited to see him. She was prepared to sacrifice her field glasses—'they cost £14'—for the war effort.

In 1940 she volunteered to do some envelope-stuffing for Dr Ryle, who was standing for Parliament as an Independent in the days (before 1950) when the University had its own MP. There were 39,000 election addresses to be sent. 'They are a very nice family,' she reported, 'and have a delightful budgerigar, trained to say "Blast Hitler".' In spite of her work, Dr Ryle was not elected. (He became Regius Professor of Physic (medicine) and was the father of Martin Ryle, the future radio astronomer and Astronomer Royal.)

Rosalind showed a very proper big-sisterly concern for my schooling. I was then ten, and my school evacuation, though successful as far as I knew, had for some reason ended after one term. She researched various ideas for my future, warning of the horrors of one suggestion: 'not at all a suitable place for a respectable person to allow her sister to go to'. As it turned out, I had two further schools before ending up, like her, at St Paul's.

At Newnham there were air raid practices, stirrup pump practices, fire-watching, chaotic warning systems, and propaganda stories on the German wireless that various Cambridge colleges were in flames. Rosalind fought with some success against what she saw as unnecessary and disruptive journeys to the cold trenches. But there were also some very real bombs, notably one near the railway station, and one in Vicarage Terrace which killed nine people—thought to be the first civilian casualties of the war. The wife of the Greek professor was killed. Rosalind seemed to take air raids in her stride:

> We were all called out by whistles—the <u>most</u> immediate of all immediate danger signals. The 'fire brigade', 36 in each hall, patrolled the top floor and roof—it seemed a trifle mad to put half the inhabitants on the top floor but it was nearly over by the time we got there, and it was a lovely fine warm night. There was one fire visible, and a number of incendiaries burning themselves out, and flares.

Internment of aliens took away many lecturers—particularly from the biochemistry lab, which was in danger of closing. There was uncertainty about summer vacation courses, and about everything else:

> It seems quite possible that this place will close down next year, or, if and when chemists are wanted, that they will be given jobs on the strength of Part I, which, after all, is a degree if you choose to take 3 years over it. On the other hand, if they are not <u>yet</u> wanted enough for that, which I think probable, I think the best thing is certainly to stay here and finish if possible. In that case it appears to be essential to come up for the Long Vac Term. I think there would be no point now in settling down permanently to anything non-scientific, firstly because I should be quite exceptionally bad at all the possibilities I can think of, and secondly because an increasing supply of chemists is bound to be needed as the war proceeds.

Strange to think that, even for a moment, she should consider the possibility of leaving science. In any case, she expected to have a month at home, and she consulted our parents about the most useful way to spend it:

> As you know, land work is not my speciality. Do you think I could find something to do in London during that time? I don't know what is going on, but I imagine there must be plenty—refugee depots or canteens or something. Will you make some suggestions.

She did stay for her third year in college, and success in her exams (in spite of the usual worry that she had done poorly) had even brought her a college exhibition. She had disciplined herself to work hard by deliberately leaving her pen in the library 'so that I can be sure I go back and work instead of wasting time in my room'.

Meanwhile, the war news brought nothing but gloom:

> What do you mean exactly when you say 'we shall win, both on grounds of common sense and of faith'? I don't see how either of those can win the war, and evil forces have often triumphed in the past—you will say, only temporarily, but it is poor comfort to think that we may be beaten but some day will be resurrected. Common sense, at present, I should say would definitely lead one to say that we are being beaten. It is a long time since we have had any good news. Any belief that we will win must, I think, be founded principally on our far greater ultimate resources. Incidentally, America is not likely to let us lose, though she seems willing to let us come very near it…All this does <u>not</u> mean that I think permanently of nothing but the war as you seem to. <u>Do</u> write something else sometimes. I couldn't bear to live in such a permanently depressed condition.

That summer (1940) she spent a few days with family friends in Sussex, where she saw rather too much of the air battles:

> We saw three planes come down. One, a Spitfire, 2 or 3 miles away we saw plainly spinning through the air, and a parachute appeared and opened just in time. Then there was the one I told you about, which was really too close to be pleasant. A Spitfire diving and turning about 100 ft over the house, apparently crashing into the house, but actually shooting at a German which had just passed over.

As London bombing got steadily worse, our house lost its windows and Notting Hill became a difficult place to live; 'I think everybody I know here who comes from London has lost at least windows, and some roofs and walls,' Rosalind wrote. After searching for somewhere safer but not too far away, my parents rented an unfurnished house in Radlett, Hertfordshire, and asked Rosalind what belongings they should take for her:

> I don't think you mentioned my desk. If it does not go, I would like everything out of it, in as little muddle as possible—I know exactly where everything in it is, though it may look confused. Also nearly everything from the drawers of my bookcase, and my climbing boots from the cupboard underneath I couldn't bear to have them bombed…Also my rucksack…As for books, I don't think there are any I can say I 'specially want', but I would like, naturally, to have as many with me as possible. One cannot live in a house permanently without books…In particular, I might mention all French books, my French dictionary, and encyclopedia—though this doesn't mean that I don't want any others.

Air raid precautions in Newnham became, according to Rosalind, increasingly farcical, and began to have a Marx Brothers touch:

> I (and more than half the college) are in the 'fire brigade'. The organisation's hopeless, but we had an extremely good lecture on incendiaries. There are now at least three sorts of air raid warning in the day-time—the siren, a signal from the Observer Corps to the Post Office, to which Newnham and most other large establishments are connected, and the roof-spotters. The first two <u>never</u> occur at the same time, and the 3rd, of course, only functions during the siren warning, but doesn't coincide with the 'buzzer'. The buzzer goes in our hall, and if it goes during a meal, we have to disperse—only because the hall is very crowded at meals. The only time this happened was one day when I overslept, and arrived at breakfast at 9 o'clock. There were only 6 of us there, but the buzzer went, and we had to 'disperse' and lost our breakfast.

The war brought one bonus to Rosalind—the arrival in Newnham of a French Jewish refugee scientist with her schoolgirl daughter. Adrienne Weill was, Rosalind wrote, 'a delightful person, full of good stories, and most interesting to talk to on any scientific or political subject'. Concerned for refugees and always drawn to anyone French, Rosalind found Adrienne's company stimulating:

> Last week I went to a talk (in French) by a Mme Weill on Mme Curie. She is a French physicist—'eminent' we are told, who came out in response to de Gaulle's appeal for scientific specialists, and has been 'adopted' by Newnham and is now researching in the Cavendish. She was a pupil of Mme Curie, and later researched with her in her lab. I was really thrilled by the lecture.

'I've met some interesting French friends of hers,' she added to David. It also turned out that Adrienne's mother, a distinguished philosopher, had known our great-uncle, Herbert Samuel, quite well, and had also stayed for some months with a feminist great-aunt of ours (presumably the formidable Netta).

With her daughter Marianne, Adrienne was, as it happened, one of many examples of a successful scientist who was also a successful mother. This made her an excellent role model, for Rosalind never decided that science and marriage were incompatible and that her life was to be devoted only to science.

Adrienne became, both personally and scientifically, an important part of Rosalind's life in Cambridge and in Paris. Living in Paris was still far in the future, and Rosalind's current worry was to do well in her exams and get a research grant. The alternative was bleak. Someone from the Appointments Board gave a talk at Newnham saying they would all have to go onto the Central Register and that in Rosalind's case this would lead to work as an 'experimental assistant' in the Ministry of Supply. 'It sounds deadly dull.'

'I have worked far less well this term than last year,' she wrote miserably at the beginning of May, 'partly because it is more difficult work, but chiefly, I think, because three times is too much, and I just can't get all worked up over it again though it matters far more this time.' But she certainly did get all worked up; the stress brought sleeplessness, and a bad cold compounded the problems. Rosalind had desperately wanted another first but after making 'a terrible mess of things' she got an upper second. Frederick Dainton, who had supervised her in that final year, was not too surprised—he thought she had a first-class brain, but was too inclined to pursue subjects that interested her deeply, to the comparative neglect of others. It may be an excellent feature for a scientist, but it may not lead to excellent exam results. It took her a long time to get over the exam trauma; it was not till nearly the end of the next term that she could write:

> My interest in chemistry is beginning to revive at last—I hope it lasts so that after Christmas I can really settle down to work intelligently. I am beginning to feel that I want to read and make up for all I haven't read in the last six months. All of which only shows the iniquities of the examination system—it has taken me over six months to begin to recover from the mental exhaustion of last June.

Anyway, with the support of Dainton's belief in her abilities, she had got her important research grant. Perhaps it is worth noting that Francis Crick had got only a second class degree in physics from University College London (having failed to get into Cambridge), and Maurice Wilkins had got only a second class degree in physics from Cambridge.

CHAPTER 5

A False Start

R osalind's first experience of research turned out to be a bitter disappointment.

Her time as a Cambridge research student was brief. She was working under the Professor of Physical Chemistry Ronald Norrish, a distinguished scientist who later won a Nobel Prize (1967), so all seemed promising. But Rosalind felt the problem he gave her had nothing to do with war work, was not worth doing, and, on top of everything, that his interpretation was in fact wrong (and Dainton agreed with her). Norrish had something of a reputation for resenting opposition from his juniors, particularly from women, and, as his biographers admit, could be 'obstinate and almost perverse in argument, overbearing and sensitive to criticism'.[1] With her uncompromising honesty (and lack of tact), Rosalind made her views quite clear from the start. 'Norrish is a very difficult man to work under,' she complained in a letter home in December,

I'm only just beginning to realise how well justified his bad reputation is. Well I've now got thoroughly on the wrong side of him, and almost reached a deadlock. He's the sort of person who likes you all right as long as you say yes to everything he says and agree with all his mis-statements, and I always refuse to do that. He tells me I mustn't take any step without asking him and has now run out of ideas and tells me to go back and try the first method again (after I proved three months ago that it didn't work). I refused, and we parted angry, and I've been working it off on various people all the afternoon, finishing up on you. Again I've got vague hopes of better things in the future. Dainton has been promised a research student to work for him, and will have me if ever the promise is fulfilled—but the promise was made a year ago, and he made me the same offer in August and it never came off. He has a first-class brain and would be a good person to work under, but is also very much on the wrong side of Norrish so isn't likely to be able to help much at present.

It was a bad experience of lab politics. And, as even my mother wrote in her memorial pamphlet, 'Rosalind's hates, as well as her friendships, tended to be enduring'. Norrish and Rosalind were clearly heading for disaster. In an undated (but presumably later) letter, Rosalind wrote:

> The long-expected crisis over my work arrived in the middle of last week—and is only just beginning to subside. While it lasted I was quite incapable of thinking or writing sanely on any subject. I had proved to the satisfaction of myself and Dainton that my reaction was not at all what Norrish expected, but an every-day one which was not worth investigating further. But Norrish refused to read what I had written, and insisted that there were reasons for continuing

and when I stood up to him he became most offensive, and we had a first-class row—in fact, several.

When Rosalind died, Adrienne Weill wrote to my mother (in a phrase that was meant to be seen as a compliment) that 'she [Rosalind] was always so frank in her likings and in her dislikings'. Anyway, in a foreshadowing of her more famous relationship with Maurice Wilkins, Rosalind found herself in a misery of non-communication.

Rosalind's letters home show an increasing confidence in her own beliefs, even if not in her own work. They were often argumentative, but always basically good-tempered. Even the following letter with the statement of her creed, which has been quoted before and which may seem confrontational, ends with talk of tea parties and holidays and birthday presents. Arguments, for Rosalind, had something of the nature of an intellectual sport, with no underlying ill will. It is astonishing to see how open and forthcoming she was:

> You frequently state, and in your letter you imply, that I have developed a completely one-sided outlook, and look at everything and think of everything in terms of science. I think this is a completely distorted view. Obviously my method of thought and reasoning is influenced by a scientific training—if that were not so, my scientific training would have been a waste and a failure. But you look at science (or at least talk of it) as some sort of demoralising invention of man, something apart from real life, and which must be cautiously guarded and kept separate from everyday existence. But science and everyday life cannot and should not be separated. Science, for me, gives a partial

explanation of life. In so far as it goes, it is based on fact, experience and experiment. Your theories are those which you and many other people find easiest and pleasantest to believe, but, so far as I can see, they have no foundation other than that they lead to a pleasant view of life (and an exaggerated idea of our own importance).

To return to the question of faith. I agree that faith is essential to success in life (success of any sort) but I do not accept your definition of faith i.e. belief in life after death. In my view, all that is necessary for faith is the belief that by doing our best we shall come nearer to success and that success in our aim (the improvement of the lot of mankind, present and future) is worth attaining. Anyone able to believe in all that religion implies obviously must have such faith, but I maintain that faith in this world is perfectly possible without faith in another world…One further point. Your faith rests on the future of yourself and others as individuals, mine in the future and fate of our successors. It seems to me that yours is the more selfish.

It has just occurred to me that you may raise the question of a creator. A creator of what? I cannot argue biologically, as that is not my field.

It was to be several years before she could argue biologically.

At first she enjoyed her very unglamorous digs in Mill Road, then a very unglamorous part of Cambridge. 'It is a pleasant room, and I think things will be quite satisfactory in spite of a rather queer landlady.' There's a danger sign here, for the landlady, with her 'little meannesses and uncivilised habits', was to become a major problem. Meanwhile, Rosalind read a lot, finding new pleasure in reading during meals when she was on her own—the only book she comments on is Virginia Woolf's *To The Lighthouse* (which she disliked for the affectation of its style). Another new pleasure (a twenty-first birthday present from an aunt) was having her own wireless, a primitive affair that ran off the light socket, and was used by her almost entirely for news. She loved her independence, and having friends and family to stay. She much enjoyed a visit from Mamie, even if they did talk gloomily about the likelihood of a further ten years of war; they had 'a nice lazy breakfast in dressing gowns, and lunch together before she departed'. I stayed with Rosalind around that time, when I was twelve, and found her wonderful company, thoughtful, and imaginative. She took me on the river and to see the obvious Cambridge sights—but also on a trip to see the baker in Newnham village stirring a huge vat of dough, and she gave me a demonstration of the impressive glass-blowing techniques she used to construct some of her apparatus.

Always ready to go to endless trouble for her friends, she had a great capacity for enjoyment. To use a modern term, she was not 'ageist', but liked, and was liked by, aged aunts and small children. Later, her friends' children would all look forward to her visits, and many have commented on how she would bring absolutely the right toy when she came to visit, and would play with them with obvious pleasure; she herself became an excellent aunt.

She enjoyed art exhibitions, and loved the theatre as long as the plays were what she considered 'worthwhile'. But she couldn't tolerate 'whodunnits', or what she considered 'rubbish'—goodness knows what she would have thought of modern television—and she would always retreat into a disconcerting silence in the company of trivial small talk or if she felt out of tune with her surroundings. She could play with children on their own terms, but she expected more from adults. To use Lady Jebb's phrase, she was 'impatient of twaddle'. It was almost as if she knew she hadn't much time and was determined to make the most of what she had.

Turning back to her work, she had the possibility of a new project that would be a slight improvement, but she was still worried:

> I found it difficult to interest myself in formaldehyde from methane before, but I was just able to give my mind to it, but now that I know I shall probably be chucking – that is, chucking a 2 or 3 yrs job after 2 or 3 months, I simply can't even think about it seriously, and to do any work that is worth while one needs to be passionately interested in one's subject. The new subject—fluorescence of solids, with particular reference to methods of rapid analysis—is a branch which I didn't specially want to do, but is, I think, a good subject of its sort, and certainly preferable to my present one.

She did make the change, and felt there was some improvement, but she was still unsatisfied:

> I've changed my job, which is satisfactory, although I haven't got the one I really wanted. The new problem should take only 6 months or so and be rather straightforward—the continuation of someone else's work—and then I should go on to some related problem.

The decision to chuck 'a 2 or 3 yrs job after 2 or 3 months' can't have been easy and the change, even with the hope of 'some related problem', still didn't make the progress of her career straightforward or obvious. The possibility of conscription added to the uncertainty. And the pleasures of living on her own soon faded—Rosalind was too social by nature to enjoy it for long. Her Newnham contemporaries had scattered, and although there were visitors, there were also long gaps. She was able to see little of Anne or Jean, her school friends, at that time, though they were to reappear often later in her life. Loyalty to friends was always a fine feature of her nature; both Anne and Jean have shown the importance to them of her friendship in the memorial tributes they have written. In that year, four years after leaving St Paul's, she was asking me for the date of the summer 'old girls' meeting.

In a bad mood in the early summer Rosalind wrote home:

> I live alone, and most of my friends have gone—all the friends that remain go down for good this month. I am intensely bored with my work, I despise my professor. I dislike the men who work in my lab, and they resent and generally ignore my presence.

There's always a danger that letters, particularly spontaneous letters like Rosalind's, may represent the mood of the moment, more than a permanent view of life, but the misery here, though not necessarily in such an extreme form, did persist. It's not really surprising that my father sometimes felt that Rosalind might be happier and better employed if she gave up the idea of a career in science.

The friend who rescued Rosalind, and turned a difficult year into at least a social success at the end, was Adrienne. She was, by then, running a hostel for foreign students in Mill Lane, just across the river from Newnham, and she suggested Rosalind might join. Rosalind was doubtful at first: 'I like people so much better when I don't live with them,' she wrote home, 'and if you live with people all the time you can't have friends who clash with them. Many of my friends this year hate each other—you see, I'm more tolerant than most, in spite of your fixed notion that I'm intolerant.' That was written in May, and the move happened in June. The international atmosphere was what Rosalind needed, and her time there, though so brief, was definitely a success. Before the move she had written of:

> an expedition with a delightful French party. I don't know whether I meet here a particularly select French crowd, but I always revel in their company. Their standard of everyday conversation is vastly superior to that of any English gathering I have been in—they are all so much more quick-witted and alive, and I love listening to their language, though I find myself quite unable to take part—the pace is much too fast for me.

In June a startling letter came from the Ministry of Labour saying that all women research students, whatever their work, were to be 'de-reserved', that is, they were now liable to be directed into war work of some sort. Rosalind was anxious to stay in Cambridge if possible, and Norrish was clearly unexpectedly sorry to let her go, yet work under Norrish did not seem in any way

FIG. 14. 12 Mill Lane, where Adrienne Weill had her hostel (photo Sarah Glynn).

worthwhile, and the pretence (as she saw it) that what she was doing was war work, bothered her very honest nature.

> What I am offered here is definitely a second-rate job, with a vague offer of better and independent work when a suitable problem presents itself. In industry there undoubtedly are better jobs, but the trouble is they never go to women. If it is only a matter of a year or so it doesn't much matter which I choose, but if it's five or ten it would probably be better here—I should eventually be doing more independent work. If I choose industry, the past year would probably count for nothing, and it's very unlikely I should ever come back here. As you see, I favour Cambridge if only I can be persuaded that the job offered is reasonable. As long as one stays in a university, even on utilitarian work, it is

science for knowledge. I'm so afraid that in industry I should find only science for money.

She had been unlucky in the research job she had been given in Cambridge, and it might have been rash to decide to give it up, but she was wonderfully lucky in the job she found connected with industry. It was definitely war work, it gave her the opportunity she needed for independent worthwhile research, and it started her on the path she was to follow for her whole career.

CHAPTER 6

Winning the War, with Coals and Carbons

The British Coal Utilisation Research Association (BCURA), where Rosalind was to work for the next four years, had been founded only in 1938. The director of research was Dr Donald Bangham, who made a point of recruiting young graduate chemists and physicists to tackle a range of carbon problems. He was, according to the BCURA 1942 report, looking more for 'a knowledge of the latest techniques developed in such leading schools as the Cavendish Laboratory', than for 'previous knowledge of coal or coal combustion'. BCURA still exists, but only funds various projects and seminars, and no longer has its own labs. Its website has no mention of the names Bangham or Franklin, though Rosalind's work there was to become famous and, together with her continuing work on carbons in Paris, is still cited and honoured by workers in the field.

In 1942, the BCURA lab offered Rosalind worthwhile war work, the opportunity to produce a Ph.D. thesis (although the work was scarcely connected to her abortive year of research in Cambridge), and an encouraging research atmosphere with a freedom in every way different from work under Norrish. Despite all this, she felt a bit hesitant in accepting:

> I've said I'll do it if they want me, and I should hear soon. I think the work sounds not too bad, but I don't like the idea of the place [Kingston-on-Thames]—miles from anything, without even the consolation of a lunch-hour in town—it'll be lunch in the lab with lab people, all horribly shut off. But the alternatives are probably worse.

She was not sorry to leave her Cambridge job, but she was sorry to leave Adrienne's international hostel. She may also have missed teaching—she had written in a letter from her research year in Cambridge that the one 'bright spot' had been two hours a week giving tutorials. And the Cambridge college system had made her used to varied company, not just 'lab people'. There is always something of a shock on leaving a university, and Kingston, just outside London, was, as she said, 'miles from anything', not at all promising.

Some social variety came from her living arrangements. We had left Radlett when the Blitz was over, and moved back to Pembridge Place. She joined us there temporarily, but the journey was tiresomely long and she had learnt the need for independence. The problem was solved by her cousin Irene, recently down from Bristol University, where she had been reading chemistry. Irene was living, with a university friend, in the basement of her parents' empty house on Putney Common, in south London; her parents had left wartime London for Chartridge. It was a house Rosalind knew well, for she had visited there often, and had stayed there as a schoolgirl in 1936, when our parents were briefly away. There was plenty of room for three, and the ménage lasted successfully until Irene's marriage to a Czech refugee doctor two years later. The household was completed by a black and white kitten; Rosalind liked cats but was doubtful about dogs—my mother always had a dog, and hoped that we would grow up to do the same, but none of us did. Once, when her flatmates were away and Rosalind needed company, I stayed there for a week, enjoying the casual organization and the atmosphere, and impressed at the way she produced good meals with the minimum of time and effort. We were glad Rosalind seemed happy, and that her work was obviously satisfying—though we had very little idea of its importance or of her growing distinction.

Research into the best use of coal had obvious wartime importance. So with David bravely moving to join the parachute corps, and Colin in the navy, my father could feel that the family was properly employed. He himself, managing his banking business in the mornings, was spending the afternoons, unpaid, at the Ministry of Home Security, concerned with the distribution of Morrison shelters—indoor steel cages (named after the then Home Secretary, Herbert Morrison), designed to give protection from falling debris. My mother was running a clothing depot for refugees, and a war-work party among the wives at the Working Men's College, knitting warm clothes and distributing books for the students in the forces. She also kept up a personal correspondence with all those students, helping the College start up again after the war. Roland and I were both still at school. Roland was to join the navy in 1944, but never saw active service.

Living in London in the early 1940s was often not easy. Rosalind and Irene both became air-raid wardens, checking that 'blackouts' in the district were adequate, being on duty at the wardens' post for two-hour stretches, going out for emergencies. Crossing Putney Common for her duties, at night during air raids, was a worse ordeal for Rosalind than we realized at the time—sometimes in the distress of her last illness it haunted her dreams.

When Irene married, Rosalind came to Pembridge Place once again, not really happy either with the journey or with living at home. My father was pleased, though, writing to Colin that 'the house will be that much the brighter'. During the time of the flying bombs she was glad of the refuge, and also joined me most weekends at Chartridge, where I was staying with Irene and three-month-old Thomas—'rather a nice baby,' Rosalind thought. She wrote of a children's party there, the eleventh birthday of Nicholas Ragg, son of our Uncle Cecil's colleague: 'Thomas was given a piece of sugar icing. Nicholas opened Thomas's mouth, and William [Nicholas's young brother] shoved the sugar in, remarking that it was just like putting cyanide in a wasps' nest.'

Aware of our scientific ignorance, Rosalind did not communicate much about her work, but throughout the problems and bombs, it went from strength to strength.

'It is usually interesting,' she wrote to Evi in 1944, 'though I get bored at times.' There are almost no letters home from this time, because she was in London and often at home herself, so we have to wait for the rare occasions when my parents were away. At one such time there is a cheerful letter that gives something of the atmosphere of wartime London and of Rosalind's mood:

This morning I set out to buy a pair of shoes. At 9 a.m. outside Lilley & Skinner there was a queue of 200 people. So I went on to Dolcis, where there were only about 50, but after 5 minutes had passed and no one had moved in I gave up. At 10 a.m. outside Raoul, which never opens on Saturday mornings, there were 30 hopeful people waiting patiently. I tried to buy numerous other things and failed miserably though less rapidly, and eventually went to Harrods and bought some excellent chocolate peppermint creams.

The work was in fact both interesting and productive. Although there had been many advances in carbon chemistry in the first half of the twentieth century, many questions about the molecular structure of coals remained unanswered, and Rosalind was asked to focus her research on the porosity of coals. It was known that coals contain many fine pores, but how did these vary in different coals and how did these variations affect the coal's properties? Using the Heath Robinsonish apparatus shown in Fig. 15, she tackled these questions in a series of ingenious experiments.

To determine what fraction of the volume of a coal is occupied by pores, she placed a known weight of powdered coal inside a glass bulb, thoroughly evacuated the air from the bulb, and replaced it with a known amount of helium. As the helium entered the pores in the coal the pressure in the bulb dropped, and soon reached a steady level. Knowing the total amount of helium added, and its current pressure and temperature, she could calculate the volume of helium that must be in the pores. Helium was chosen for this experiment, first because it is the smallest atom available in the uncombined state, and therefore

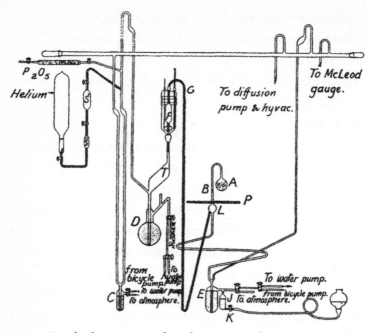

FIG. 15. Rosalind's apparatus, from her 1949 article in *Transactions of the Faraday Society* (reproduced by permission of the Royal Society of Chemistry).

very likely to be able to reach the pores, and secondly because it is entirely unreactive and therefore will not react with the coal, or be adsorbed on the internal surfaces of the coal, and so alter its properties.

She experimented using a variety of coals of increasing carbon content, from the soft brownish lignite, through sub-bituminous and bituminous coals (the commonest kind of coal), to the hardest, blackest, most lustrous anthracite. And she used not only helium but also a variety of other substances including hexane and benzene—two liquid hydrocarbons with a molecular weight about twenty times that of helium. An interesting result of experiments of this kind was that, with some coals, these hydrocarbons entered the pores much more slowly than helium, and in some cases the total volume entering was smaller. There was no suggestion of any reaction between the hydrocarbons and the coal, so it looked as though the pores were less accessible or inaccessible to large molecules, implying that access to them must involve fine constrictions whose size determines accessibility. She concluded that: 'As a result of this pore structure, the solids function as molecular sieves, the width of the constrictions in the pore system being of the same order as the diameters of the simple molecules used.'[1] Writing about Rosalind's experiments more than half a century later, Peter Harris pointed out that 'This was probably the first demonstration of molecular sieve behaviour in any carbon. Today [i.e. in 2001], carbon molecular sieves are of great value in industry where, among other things, they are used to separate nitrogen from oxygen in air.'[2] They are also sometimes used to support catalysts promoting reactions between two gases.

Carbonization—the heating of coal in the absence of air—yields three useful products: combustible gases, tar, and coke; and the coke can be used both as a fuel and as a reducing agent for extracting iron from its ores. It is therefore not surprising that Rosalind extended her studies to look at the porosity of various coals when these coals were heated to the temperatures used in carbonization (600–1,650°C). Again there were interesting results.[3] Increasing the temperature increased the pore volume, but decreased the speed at which the pores were filled. At temperatures above 600°C the large pore volume was no longer accessible to the large hydrocarbon molecules. As the temperature was further increased the pore volume became inaccessible to successively smaller molecules, until, at temperatures above 1,000°C even the volume accessible to helium was reduced. Clearly, increasing the temperature *increased* the pore volume but *narrowed* the passages through the constrictions, making part (or even the whole) of the pore volume inaccessible to molecules above a certain size.

All this work made it possible to classify coals and to predict their behaviour with remarkable accuracy, and it would give Rosalind plenty to write about in her Ph.D. thesis. But it couldn't account for the differences between the coals in terms of differences in their molecular structure. That would have to wait for the X-ray diffraction work she was to learn in Paris.

While the war was still on, Rosalind's holidays were confined to Britain, but she made the most of them. Jean Kerslake has described their hazardous walking tours where 'we should have been roped, but did not realise it at the time'. As Rosalind wrote rather alarmingly to David from Snowdonia in 1944:

> Previously on mountain holidays I had rather tended to follow paths marked on the map or other obvious tracks, but now we look at a mountain face and decide whether we can tackle it. It is much more interesting, one sees much more exciting parts, and one gets to know the mountains better.

Her school friend Anne was not as rash or as tough as Rosalind and Jean. Walking in Wales, she wrote that she was thankful when a mist came down so that she could no longer see the steep drop on either side. 'I just managed to make my way along the ridge—driven more by my fear of Rosalind's tongue than of falling over the edge.'

In June 1945, with the war in Europe over, Rosalind was given three weeks in a 'lovely large room overlooking the garden' in Newnham while she started to write up her thesis. The atmosphere was seductive. There was tennis and independence—both things that she valued—and she had time to think about her next move: 'I am seriously considering applying to the Ministry of Labour for permission to take up my studentship here for a year while I look around for a university teaching job.'

She dithered:

I am certainly enjoying the weather, the libraries, and Cambridge. I change my mind almost hourly about the future, but pottering between Newnham garden and the Philosophical Library convinces me that I can't return to CURA for an indefinite period. I am seeing Miss Curtis (the Principal) tomorrow. I'm told that it is, in general, possible for people over 25 to revert to University work. I am, of course, terribly tempted to return here. I have had a polite interview with Norrish and was completely convinced that I could never work under him again, although he offered me a place, but I could probably get into the Colloid Dept if I wanted to. But, firstly I feel that my present views on Cambridge must be highly coloured by the weather and by the complete freedom and independence of my present condition. And secondly I think that where I have tried and failed once I would stand a great chance of failing again, and it would be better to break new ground.

Failed? She was still suffering from the misery of her first experience of research. She investigated, unproductively, a junior lectureship at Bedford College (to get teaching experience as a route to other possible university jobs) and a lectureship at Aberdeen. Frustratingly, her achievements at BCURA had not yet been published—her first paper, written jointly with Bangham, did not appear until 1946. It was the first of her impressive series of papers on coals and carbons; four more (with Rosalind the sole author of three) resulted from work done at BCURA, and there were to be a further sixteen (mostly on her work in Paris) in the course of her life.

After ten days, the enthusiasm for writing her thesis had started to fade: 'Work is not progressing as I could wish.' She felt the need for another two months and became gloomy about the outcome: 'The more I write, the more I realise how incredibly dull it all is, and I'm not very optimistic about the result.'

Luckily, this was to be her last exam. In spite of her usual depression, it ended triumphantly. None of us read her thesis or could have understood it, but we were enormously proud of her Ph.D., something no one in the family had tackled before.

The war was over, so travel to France became possible again, and Rosalind was an insatiable traveller—'I cannot understand or explain how much it all interests and pleases me. I just love wandering round and chatting where possible or just sitting and gazing and absorbing my surroundings.' The whole business of studying maps and planning was a pleasure. Not in the least put off by a letter telling her that 'the French youth hostels are generally too uncomfortable. They can only fit very sportive persons who are free of any prejudice', she and Jean were happily off to the French Alps. Writing much later about this trip, Jean described how they went by local buses, which were dangerously over-crowded, with passengers travelling on the roof with the luggage. All the bridges had been blown up during the war and the new ones were temporary and very frail, so that every time we came to one we all had to get off the bus and cross the bridge on foot. At Val d'Isère we found that the Grand Hotel Parisien was a very modest establishment, very friendly but a little surprised to find two English girls travelling alone. We started by booking a guide to climb the Tsanteleina, but although we were up and ready at 4 a.m., the guide did not arrive, saying later that the weather was not good enough. We then began to go out on our own, for what we thought were fairly modest walks near the village. However, we were ill-equipped for this… On a slope above Val d'Isère Rosalind slipped and found herself spread-eagled on a fall of scree which threatened to slide over a precipice if disturbed. She dared not move, but fortunately I managed to pull her off. We then began to realise that we were taking far too many risks. Luckily, at this point we met Michael Roberts who took us out shopping and supervised the purchase of ice-axes and ropes. He taught us how to use them, told us exactly which climbs we could do on our own, and took us up the Grand Sassière.[4]

Michael Roberts (1902–48), described by his publisher Faber and Faber as 'a left-wing humanist, scientist, poet, mountaineer' (and the father of the historian of Africa, Andrew Roberts), became their friend and tutor. Rosalind wrote to him gratefully:

All your advice, suggestions and directions have been quite invaluable. We both fell in love with the hotel at the Col de l'Iséran and felt that the night there was one of the most worth while things we have done. We got two good mountains out of it, and the food was magnificent. Between us we seem to have remembered all the relevant instructions about paths, and have found everything with very little difficulty. We are also extremely glad of the rope and piolets [ice axes], which we would never have had the courage to buy without your backing.

Rosalind was surprisingly ignorant, too, about birds or flowers, though this did not prevent her enjoyment of them (she had studied chemistry and physics, not biology or botany). One of her few complaints about post-war Paris was to be the lack of crocuses or other spring flowers in the parks. At Newnham, before such behaviour was frowned on, she picked armfuls of cowslips and bluebells for her room; collecting oxlips ended in 'disillusionment when I got home and discovered that oxlips smell foul'. 'If I knew anything about flowers, which I don't,' she wrote from the Alps in the August of 1946,

> I would write for weeks about the flowers on the mountains. The variety and the colour are amazing. The most impressive, perhaps, is the mass of blue jenshuns (my spelling being phonetic), the colour of which is really startling. Otherwise things like pale mauve crocuses, French marigolds, deep purple hairbells, Woolworths cactuses, all sorts of rock plants, thistles the size of cabbages, and heaven knows what. Also masses of exotic butterflies and grasshoppers and flying beetles, but I don't know anything about any of them.

Once, I remember, she sent me an edelweiss—'they are not particularly beautiful, but I feel it is quite the right thing to send home'.

The holiday had been exciting and stimulating, but what next? She was reluctant to go back to BCURA, felt restless, ready for change. She would have liked to move back to university life or with great luck just possibly, in a post-war world, to get a research job in France. It seemed a remote hope that France could become a place for work, not simply a wonderful place for holidays. In this state of indecision she wrote in the spring of 1946, only half-seriously and without much optimism, to Adrienne:

> If ever you hear of anybody anxious for the services of a physical chemist who knows very little about physical chemistry but a lot about the holes in coal, please let me know.

It may have been a shot in the dark, but it was an extraordinarily lucky one. Adrienne once more became her saviour, telling her that at the conference on carbon that was to take place at the Royal Institution that autumn there would be two French scientists, Marcel Mathieu and Jacques Mering, both friends of hers, who would like to meet Rosalind and might be able to help her. Rosalind presented a paper at the conference, asked intelligent questions, and showed the visiting Frenchmen round London. They were impressed. Mathieu, a communist with a great wartime reputation as a Resistance fighter, had a powerful position in French science, and it was through him that Rosalind found herself, in February 1947, a *chercheur* in the Laboratoire Central des Services Chimiques de l'État, at 12 quai Henri IV.

CHAPTER 7

Happiness in Paris

Rosalind was to have four happy years in Paris.

She was twenty-six when she arrived, and single. Paris has always had a reputation as a romantic city, so there have been various suggestions about her possible romantic life there—but all of them are wrong; her happiness came simply from a love of the place, from friendships, and from fulfilment in her work.

The BBC TV *Horizon* programme implied a relationship with Vittorio Luzzati; in fact, although they were colleagues and always remained excellent friends, they were certainly no more than that. Since there was no future there, Jacques Mering, Rosalind's supervisor, was later suggested as a candidate; he, as it happens, already had a wife and a mistress. Rosalind admired Mering as a scientist, and she must have felt a pang of nostalgia when he rang her and came to see her later in her illness. He reportedly wept after seeing her—as he might have done after seeing any young talented pupil close to death. It is wrong to read any more than that into their relationship.

Luzzati shared Rosalind's taste for heated discussion and argument—Anne Sayre records a colleague saying, 'When Vittorio and Rosalind were together, it was hammer and tongs and quite exhausting'. And Vittorio and his wife Denise also shared her taste for the countryside and energetic holidays. Rosalind joined them on their great bicycle tour in Tuscany in 1950—'unforgettable' as Vittorio Luzzati wrote—in a countryside as yet untouched by tourists. It is still a good memory for him. The well-known happy photograph of Rosalind looking out over a wall, with her bicycle beside her, was taken by Vittorio on this tour.

Whenever possible they would escape to the Alps, too, or all go off to the countryside at weekends.

FIG. 16. Looking over a parapet in Tuscany (photo Vittorio Luzzati).

FIG. 17. Rosalind in an Alpine hut (the Cabane des Evettes) (photo
Vittorio Luzzati).

In the summer of 1947 Rosalind had been back in the Alps
with Jean, for one of her best walking holidays. They went,
Rosalind wrote to Colin, on

> the most heavenly expedition I have ever done … We started out
> in cloud at 4.30 a.m., and the cloud lifted suddenly at sunrise,
> just as we came onto the glacier, revealing pink summits above a
> 'mer de nuages'. I cannot describe the effects, I can only tell you
> that the sheer beauty of it made me weep.

Another walk from Pralognan la Vanoise, which still amazes
any who know the district, involved tackling the Grande Casse,
the biggest local mountain, and ended, as if it were the most
normal thing in the world, in catching the night train back to
Paris and work:

I found it no effort at all. We walked up to the Refuge Fèlix Faure the evening before in 2 hrs 10 mins, a walk, from 1400 to 2500 metres, described in the guide books as 3 1/2 hours. We were surrounded by the fiercest mountain storms, dark yellow cloud and flashes all round, though we ourselves kept reasonably dry. We went up in spite of the weather because it was my last day, and we decided to have a shot at it in the morning if the weather was anything but hopeless. By the time we had finished dinner the sky had cleared. We set out at 3.30 a.m. in the dark, a most perfect night, slowly tramping up the lower slopes behind the guide's lantern. A fine night at 3000 metres has to be seen to be believed. As we got up on to the rocks, and a little later on to the glacier, day began to break. First the distant snow begins to show up clearly, then dark red streaks appear gradually in the sky all around. These get brighter and more extensive for some time, the atmosphere is full of suspense, and finally there is the wonderful moment, which has been so often described, when the sun flashes on to the mountain tops over the whole wide landscape and rapidly covers the whole earth with the dazzling early morning pink. There were only three of us, the guide, a pleasant Belgian medical student who had spent the war in England, and myself. Soon after sunrise we were up over the glacier and the rocks on to the long final ridge which leads to the summit—the ridge mainly rock, with an impressive stretch of narrow snow ridge near the top. 8 a.m. on the summit we settled down to the extra mountain meal which has no name. (Breakfast at 3 a.m., lunch at the refuge at 1.p.m., the expedition having to be over early because melting snow later in the day is troublesome to walk on and, more serious, brings danger of falling rocks.) The day was perfect, and we seemed more central and better placed than ever for a superb view of all the Alps of France, Switzerland and Italy. About 9 we left for the most satisfying descent I have ever done. The Belgian led down over the rocks very competently, and on the glacier, and later the stony moraine below, I was astonished at my ability to run and slide down in sharp zigzags with the guide, leaving our Belgian friend far behind on the moraine. It is the most wonderful feeling when one's body does absolutely all that is required of it on such an occasion with no jarring or effort. It felt more like a descent on skis.

Down at the refuge at mid-day to lunch, and a rapid walk down to Pralognan.

The summer of 1948 brought a different and lazier journey, a holiday in Corsica with Colin and a group of twelve or so from the Paris lab. Calvi was beautiful; Rosalind loved the new sights, the colours, and the underwater world, and she was able to explore the island in energetic walks with Colin.

The following year she was off to Italy with an Australian scientist, Margaret Nance:

Margaret and I go very well together—considering she'd never seen a mountain before she's taken to it extraordinarily well. She gets up hill a bit better than me, I get down a bit better. I'm a bit braver about walking along ridges, and she's wonderfully brave about taking the worms out of my pears and peaches.

When Margaret left, Rosalind was off back to the Alps, sending home the sort of letter that is better to receive after the event than before:

The first day the Castor, by a steep icy slope on the north side— the guide telling me that the normal gentler route was 'pas pour alpinistes'. The next day was the big day, over the two Lyskamms

(4540 m.), a long walk along ice ridges [a ridge first traversed in 1864 by a group of four including Leslie Stephen] and up to the Cabane Margherita, 4560 m., for the night. But, as is apparently very normal, after a night at that height I was not feeling fit for another mountain next day, so we spent it coming down by stages, first over the glacier to the Sella hut again, and eventually to Champoluc, where I spent the night, collected my luggage, ate a welcome meal, and left at 6 a.m.

Even reading this is exhausting, and it's not surprising, though it is impressive, to read on:

For the second time in my career (the first was at Pralognan) the guide asked me to come back next year and do a 'première ascension' with him! I replied, of course, that 'premières ascensions' were not in my line and he could go and do it by himself, to which he retorted that he wouldn't get the same publicity.

Letters flowed, because family bonds remained strong, and Rosalind's new life should in no way be seen as a move to get away. Independence in work and in her life mattered to her, but so did her roots, and her friendship with her brothers and with me. She even endured a long uncomfortable train journey one night to join us all for a brief few days and a visit to the Lascaux caves when we holidayed in France. Family visits were important, in both directions; she loved it when family visited her, she came home regularly, and made extra trips for her brothers' weddings, David's in May 1947, Roland's in June 1949, and Colin's in January 1950. There were limits to her cooperation though: 'I will *not* get a new hat. I've only got 3 brothers, and I don't consider 3 outings excessive for one hat.'

The letters changed with time, not because Rosalind changed, as in her four years at Cambridge, but because Paris was recovering from shortages and from wartime occupation. They are spontaneous, as if she was talking, as her letters always were, even from the days of her outpourings as a nine-year-old schoolgirl at Lindores. But although they seem to give very full accounts of her life in Paris, with plenty about her living conditions or holiday plans or her views on French politics, they never discuss her work except to say vaguely that it is going well, or needs more time, and that she values the independence she is given in the lab. She wrote to David, soon after she had arrived:

> It is too early yet to say how the work will go, as I have not got beyond the reading stage…The resources of the lab are very limited, but I am otherwise remarkably free in my work. Of course, freedom is the thing I appreciate most in this new life. It is what I came for and I have found it. My living conditions are extremely primitive compared with home—though they might well be worse. I wash in a little tin bowl, the only water being from one cold tap in the kitchen the other end of the flat. I have lunch out and buy cold food to eat in my room in the evenings. And I have practically no heating—fortunately I had some wood to burn in the coldest weather, but I am unable to get any more, but I would willingly go more primitive if it were necessary to preserve my freedom…Paris is very lovely even in winter. I get a fresh thrill every day when I walk to or from my work along by the Seine.

Colin and I joined the lab lunch party one day, in the picturesque small restaurant they all patronized. Bread came flying

through the air, plate sizes were graded according to the food—
large for meat, smaller for vegetables—and the bill was calcu-
lated by counting the number of different plates each person
had accumulated.

A couple of years later, a letter to my father tried to explain
the point of it all:

> You enquire about the importance of my job. Perhaps it misleads
> you that it is called a job. The place where I work is purely a
> research establishment, and my particular work has no immedi-
> ate industrial objective (some people would call it 'pure research',
> while others argue that there is no such thing as 'pure research',
> since all scientific advancement is ultimately useful). The posi-
> tion, therefore, is that I am paid and given facilities to work on
> my own ideas—and anybody else's I may be able to borrow. Its
> importance depends, of course, on what I make of it—what
> results I get, if any.

Beyond that, she must have felt the family would neither understand nor really be interested. Reading these family letters gives
no clue to the impressive stream of papers she was producing,
eleven of them published between 1949 and 1951. It was perhaps
not until she wrote home from America, from a Gordon Conference in 1954, that the family realized the importance of what
she had been doing:

> In the carbon world, [she wrote then] 'the work I did in Paris
> seems to form the background to a large part of the industrial
> research going on here, and I'm welcomed as an 'authority' on
> the subject. So much so, that I had a nightmare in which I was
> surrounded by solemn middle-aged Americans all saying 'and

what we should like to ask your opinion about next Miss Franklin is...' and then I woke up.

Her work was an extension of her work at BCURA. To investigate the microstructure of coals she needed to use X-ray diffraction, and she was now in the right place, in a unit studying carbons, with Jacques Mering to teach her the techniques she needed.

The idea of using X-ray diffraction to determine microstructure had arisen in 1912, when a German theoretical physicist, Max von Laue, was talking to a colleague in the English Garden at Munich.[1] The colleague had been attempting to investigate the structure of crystals by observing the way they diffracted visible light. Because crystals have a very regular structure, with the constituent atoms precisely placed, it seemed likely that a narrow beam of light striking the crystal would be diffracted into a number of beams of different intensities and different directions, both of which could be recorded by surrounding the crystal with a photographic film. By taking such photographs, with different orientations of the crystal, the experimenter might be able to calculate the arrangement of atoms that would give rise to the observed patterns, or, at least, to decide whether any particular pattern was compatible with the set of photographs. Talking in the Munich garden, it occurred to von Laue that, given the smallness of the inter-atomic distances likely to be found in crystals, it might be better to use X-rays rather than light rays, because their wavelengths are much smaller. Two weeks spent experimenting with crystals of copper sulphate proved he was right.

In 1913, using X-rays, the Braggs, father and son, showed that diamonds—one crystalline form of pure carbon—consisted of carbon atoms arranged tetrahedrally and held together by co-valent bonds. In 1924 Bernal showed that graphite—another crystalline form of pure carbon—consisted of stacked sheets, with the atoms in each sheet arranged in hexagons, but with no covalent bonds between the sheets, so that graphite could easily be cleaved into flakes. Rosalind, though, was faced with a more difficult problem because the materials she was interested in were not fully crystalline, and had a more limited internal order. She worked with a variety of carbon compounds including coals and other solid organic compounds (including plastics), and she made 'many improvements in X-ray diffraction meth-ods for imaging large complex molecules, and in the accompa-nying mathematical techniques'.[2]

The results were interesting and unexpected. She found that, depending on their chemical composition, the materials she was studying fell into two groups, which differed in their response to prolonged heating in the absence of air. One group soon yielded carbons (she called them graphitizing carbons) that, on further heating, readily converted into graphite. The other group, even with prolonged heating at high temperatures, yielded carbons (she called them non-graphitizing carbons) that were very hard despite their low density, and were highly porous though the pores were accessible only through narrow constrictions.

Analysis of the X-ray diffraction patterns of the graphitizing and non-graphitizing carbons showed a striking difference in structure. Both consisted of small subunits that resembled tiny crystals of graphite, each with just a few layer planes. But the arrangement of these subunits was very different. In the graphitizing carbons, neighbouring subunits were always roughly parallel with each other, and because the subunits remained relatively mobile during the early stages of carbonization, it looked as though the linkages between them were weak. With roughly parallel subunits and weak links between them, conversion into graphite presents no obvious difficulties. In contrast, the subunits in the non-graphitizing carbons were randomly oriented, and the striking hardness of these carbons suggested that the linkages between the subunits were strong. With random orientation and strong linkages, conversion to graphite would be difficult.

Although Rosalind was not herself involved in the industrial use of her work on carbons, Aaron Klug, writing in the *Oxford Dictionary of National Biography*, points out that her results 'proved to be highly relevant for the development of carbon fibres, materials of industrial importance which are made of rolled up parallel sheets of graphite layers'.[3] These fibres are both much stronger and much lighter than steel, and their major application is in reinforcing plastics to form composites which, as structural materials, are used in the newest generation of airliners, high-performance cars, and sports goods. The non-graphitizing carbons have also proved useful as glassy material, sold as 'vitreous carbon', for making laboratory apparatus that needs to be chemically resistant and withstand very high temperatures.[4]

A few years ago a young cousin, working in coal research, was amazed at what he found in the literature; he suggested there should be an English Heritage blue plaque in Rosalind's memory, and that it should mention her work on carbons and her later work on viruses as well as her work on DNA. The plaque is there now, on Rosalind's later London flat in Drayton Gardens on the borders of Chelsea and Fulham, with the comprehensive words 'Pioneer of the study of molecular structures including DNA'.

In Paris she never had her own flat, and her living conditions, 'very primitive' as she had told David, contrasted strongly with the sophistication and distinction of her work. She felt herself lucky to have a room found for her by Adrienne, in a flat belonging to Mme Dumas, a professor's widow. The best feature was that it was in a wonderful position, in the rue Garancière, near the church of St Sulpice, and very convenient for the lab—a quarter of an hour by bus, or half an hour's walk. She was lucky to get that room, because rooms were hard to find, but with its death mask of the professor and its collection of ancient stoves and general junk, and its one cold tap, 'it is', she wrote, 'so gloomy as to be funny'. Rosalind got on well with Albertine, the maid in the flat, but found her landlady Mme Dumas rather a strain. At times Mme Dumas was away, and then Rosalind happily had baths, had guests to dinner, and even visitors to stay. My mother once braved it.

My parents worried about Rosalind's poor pay, and generally about her living conditions. But poverty is relative, and none of her colleagues were paid well, all suffered from multiple shortages, and good flats were unobtainable. As Rosalind pointed out:

One only feels rich or poor in relation to the people one mixes with, and as all my friends are in much the same position as

FIG. 18. Rue Garancière in Paris, where Rosalind had a room (photo Simon Glynn).

myself—or worse off because they have not any resources in England—I do not mind not having a lot of money to splash around in luxuries. I'm paid according to fixed laws and salary scales.

She had a different scale of values. She loved the clear air of Paris—London was still in the era of 'pea-soup' fogs—she enjoyed her journey along the Seine to the lab, the view of the Seine from the lab itself, the easy access to countryside at weekends. Above all, as she wrote home:

I find life interesting, I have good friends—though my circle is naturally smaller than in London—and I find infinite kindness and good will among the people I work with. All that is far more important than a larger meat ration or more frequent baths.

For rations and baths were indeed difficult. My parents may have been concerned at news of shortages, electricity cuts, transport strikes, but Rosalind reacted to such problems only with sympathy for underpaid workers. No one could have been less bothered about her own lack of money, as long as she had enough for food and for travel (third class, sitting up all night). Food was helped by rather basic requests to English visitors— dried potatoes, Bovril, Nescafé, tea, jam, powdered milk, drinking chocolate; also toothpaste, tennis balls, and 'some plain post cards—an invention un-known to the French, who only have them covered with roses or the Eiffel Tower'. Inner tubes for her bicycle were needed, and also, urgently, a connector for her bicycle pump.

Even bread was rationed:

> The standard ration is intolerably low, and I just don't know how people manage. I eat about twice the ration at present, chiefly because I'm a travailleur de force, which gives me bread, wine and cooking fat, all welcome, but especially now the bread.

One visiting cousin was, she wrote:

> rather shocked by my somewhat Bohemian existence, and particularly by absence of a bath. I tried to console him by reminding him that I could have a bath in May, but that seemed to make matters worse.

There were some basic shortages in the lab as well as in domestic life. She asked Colin to bring supplies of silicone vacuum wax and picein wax on his visit, for 'all the most elementary things are lacking and unobtainable'. 'If you succeed in that mission,' she added cheerfully, 'you will be contributing towards the science of clays, catalysts, burnt sugar and heaven knows what.'

She stayed in her Bohemian room for over two years. Not that she would not have welcomed a flat if one had been available. As she wrote:

> My prospects of finding a flat here are even dimmer than they would be in London. It would certainly be pleasant, but I know many people who have hunted for two years or more. Furnished flats are rare and very expensive. Unfurnished are much rarer, the rents are absurdly low, but a large lump sum has to be paid for the flat initially…the head of the lab says that somebody told him that I was 'très très bonne', so I took the opportunity of remarking that I wasn't paid much. As a result I expect to go up from about £5 to £6 per week! The prospect makes me feel quite rich.

There certainly were problems. Her picture of post-war Paris is thoughtful and observant. The high cost of food, together with low pay, constantly worried her, not so much for herself, but for those who had to support a family:

> I find I spend about 50% of my earnings on food alone. How people manage who earn less and have to keep a family I just can't imagine. By buying such things as eggs at 1s each and meat at 7 to 8s per pound I can feed myself reasonably well, but I don't know that I would like to be doing it with no help from England—i.e. with no tea, coffee or cocoa, no chocolate, no jam, no marmite, bovril, fish paste or equivalent, no milk. The sugar ration is about 1/4 lb weekly, cheese 2 oz, fats 2 oz (plus about 3 oz butter which I don't get until I get a French identity card which takes about 6 weeks)…All bus and metro fares have increased about 50% since I was here in the summer.

She sent her walking shoes home for mending 'as here there is one "bon" for the year for leather soles, and I have used it'. Clothes were beyond the means of many, and she was highly critical of the French government for failing to help:

> The recent economics of taxation increases are absurd because the government has not the strength to direct them to the people who have the money—i.e. those who amassed fortunes during the war, and the farmers and small shop-keepers who are doing so now. These, by the way, are the people who support de Gaulle. One sees his portrait in many small shops. Instead, new cuts hit hardest the most under-paid workers, so only increase the necessity for wage increases. In all this it is important to remember that the lower-paid workers have little more than starvation wages, and the urge for increase is an equivalent to an appeal for enough to eat—a situation which has no parallel in England…My co-workers who have no private means are either in rags or wear clothes sent by friends in America.

There was a severe transport strike during her first autumn in Paris:

> It is quite mad. I am fortunate in being situated within walking distance of most things, and in daylight I mostly cycle. But the traffic congestion is such that at times it is quicker to walk than cycle. An incredible number of vehicles of all sorts have appeared, and all attempt to heed the traffic signals has been abandoned, four streams of traffic simply fight for a passage at each cross-roads…The political situation which is aggravated by all this is tragic, the country being forced to choose between two extremes either of which will arouse bitter opposition and probably lead to disaster.

Then there were frustrations over time spent trying to get train tickets or visas. Trying to book for her holiday in the Alps in July 1947:

> I went to the station at 6 a.m. on the first day permissible for booking and found 300 people queuing for my train. So I retired and spent a very peaceful three hours alone working in the lab which is quite near, as the alternative was waiting till about midday and then perhaps not getting seats—I decided I would rather stand in the train.

The queues for Italian visas were so formidable that she decided they would have to stay in France.

One form of transport was simpler then than now—returning from a visit home she flew from London Airport after five minutes in the waiting room, and the late arrivals drove up to the plane in their cars.

But the saga of importing her sewing machine, even as late as 1949, is another good illustration of the general chaos:

> The Customs here are extremely tiresome about the sewing machine. It was seized and I've filled in dozens of forms and they told me I probably would hear in 3 months time that I can't have it and it will be sent back to England…After 2 months delay I received the minister's special permission (via his private secretary) to have it, and after that spent two whole days running from the station to the central customs place and back and round and round before finally paying 1100 francs and getting it.

On the whole, though, by 1949 things were easier. There was plenty of fruit and vegetables in the market, and most other foods in the shops—even if these were only available at a terrible price.

Presents brought back to France from a visit to England were a mixed success—a scarf for Albertine was fine and reckoned 'à la mode', but Bendicks bittermints for her colleagues at the lab were a failure—chocolate and peppermint, for the French, was (and still is) considered a 'drôle de mélange'.

The cultural side of French life was quick to recover from the war. Rosalind's French was good enough, even at the start, for her to enjoy the theatre or films, though there seems to have been also a supply of English films—*Henry V*, *Hamlet*, *Passport to Pimlico*, *Oliver Twist*. She was amused at the reaction of the French to the uncomplimentary portrait of the court of France in *Henry V*: 'I warn them, and they all say their feelings are no longer sensitive to the events of the 15th century. But they all come out saying that it really did go a bit far.'

Early in 1947 she wrote with pleasure of a wonderful exhibition of Van Gogh, imported from Holland. And again, 'there are two wonderful exhibitions of painting here—one of Flemish Primitives, and a vast one of French Impressionists'. In a letter to Colin in 1949 she analysed her feelings about Italian paintings—an interest perhaps first aroused by her school project on Florentine art:

As for seeing pictures in their natural surroundings, so to speak, I came to the conclusion that for me the only way was to see them in small unspoilt places where they originated. In the Uffizi in Florence I didn't feel that at last I was seeing Italian art in Italy, but rather that I was seeing a branch of the national gallery or the Louvre which happened to be in Florence. The Peruginos in

Perugia impressed me more than Raphael in Florence, not
because I prefer Perugino to Raphael, but because Perugia was
where he belonged. And the Giotto frescoes in Assisi impressed
me far more than all the rest.

Still, it wasn't always possible to be in the appropriate place,
and there was much to be got out of seeing what arrived in
Paris.

She gave Colin (who was planning his honeymoon) her clear
ideas about visiting countries with dubious politics:

> I'd love to see Spain but not now. You <u>can't</u> see a country without
> being aware of its politics. Even in Italy this summer I found the
> political background slightly depressing, but there at least one
> was free—and, more important the Italians were free—to say
> what one thought to all and sundry. When the English-speaking
> lad in the bus office at Perugia told me Mussolini was the great-
> est Italian there had ever been, I could answer him in public. I did
> not start political discussions, but I continued them once they
> were started. In several places I asked people what was the reac-
> tion of the Italian people when their government declared war
> on France in 1940. Almost uniformly they told me that most
> people were pleased because they believed, foolishly, that their
> country had entered on the winning side. It seemed to be a new
> idea to them that belief in victory was not an adequate justifica-
> tion for going to war.

On occasion, in France, Rosalind's highbrow tastes could slip a
bit:

> I went last night to an American roller skating show which drew
> a crowd of 30,000...first class entertainment of all kinds in

comic, acrobatic, and dancing. In particular a superb team of pantomime circus horses on roller skates.

And again, after a conference in Nancy:

> [I] went out with more conference people, dancing till 4 a.m..
> Saturday I spent mainly visiting Strasbourg labs and tasting superb Alsace wines, and Sunday I spent on the back of a motor-cycle in the Vosges, and again tasting wines.

Later she wrote, without further explanation, of having lots of work to do and 'what with that and the lighter side of things I'm pretty busy'.

A small wireless, compatible with French voltage, was badly needed, because she suffered from lack of news. There was much to see and do and write about, but concern for politics never left her. She poured out her increasingly left-wing views in her letters, as she had from Newnham. She had a horror of de Gaulle, feeling that in England no one realized that he was now almost like Oswald Mosley in his outlook, even if he had been a great Free French leader in 1940. She regretted, and thought many French regretted, the lack of a socialist middle way between communism and de Gaulle-type fascism which she thought might even result in civil war in France or lead to war with Russia. By the time de Gaulle did become prime minister of France, in May 1958, Rosalind was no longer alive.

She was also alarmed at the idea of the cold war turning into a very real one, with McCarthy emerging by 1950 as a seriously worrying figure. I do not remember feeling in Britain, at that time, that war was imminent or even possible, so it is startling to read how often, both before and during the Korean War, Rosalind writes of European war as at least likely if not inevitable—presumably a reflection of much contemporary French thought. In July 1950, for example, she was writing:

> Last week it looked as though your holiday—and everybody else's— was going to end as in 1939, and now there seems to be a general and depressing acceptance of the idea that the war has been 'postponed'.

And in the next month:

> More and more people are taking it for granted that there'll be war soon. The Americans prepare to go home. The French have cleared the shops of sugar, soap, oil, and nylon stockings—as though it mattered, if there's a war, whether one has war with or without stockings or with or without a few more kilos of sugar!

To turn from world problems to more local matters, she enjoyed learning to negotiate the problems of cycling in Paris, and she started playing tennis occasionally with Adrienne and friends on the roof of the Ecole Normale, with its great view over all Paris. She loved Paris, later calling it 'far and away the best city in the world'; she cycled along the Seine to the lab, and she enjoyed the company of her colleagues, an international group who would argue energetically about work and politics, lunch together, and go off together into the countryside for weekend walks. Rosalind's only complaint was that those walks tended to be a bit too slow and a bit too obsessed with food.

Sometimes she went on more energetic expeditions, able to indulge her love of walking and the countryside. This is from a letter written in her first summer:

> To-day has been terrifically hot, and if the weather holds I intend going out to Fontainebleau Saturday afternoon, sleeping in the forest, and walking all Sunday with a girl from Unesco [Margaret Nance]. It seems to be a popular sport (except that the French don't walk) and a good idea.

But the weather didn't hold:

> we were very lucky to find a bit of corrugated iron roofing, and also a party of five French boys who shared the roof, made a good fire, prepared the ground for sleeping, and provided soup.

Not in the least put off by their soaking, they walked twenty-five miles the next day, and she was off again the following weekend, sleeping out by the Marne:

> I personally hardly slept at all, but the air was heavenly and the night a pleasure, and at 4.30 I wandered off alone for 2 hours through the wood and further up the river. Really 4.30–5.30 a.m. is the time for seeing woods and rivers.

She had hated being in the house alone at night, either at Pembridge Place or in Putney, but it does not seem to have occurred to her that there might be anything bothering about walking in the woods alone in the early hours.

On her travels, she sometimes came across sad reminders of war. In one Alpine chalet, 6,500 feet up:

they told us that their winter dwelling at Termignon (on the line of the German retreat to the Mt Cenis tunnel) was destroyed when the town was burned down by the Germans, so now, they first go down to the valley in the usual way, driving the beasts and putting the birds (hens, ducks) on the mules, and then put the whole lot on the train to Avignon, where they rent a farm for the winter!

She reports an alarming experiment with Alpine food, but seems to have come to no harm:

I bought a cheese to bring back here. Shortly before leaving I had a look and was horrified by the mass of worms on the rind. However, I threw it into hot water, scrubbed hard, hung it out to dry in the sun, covered it with DDT and wrapped it up again, with perfect success. It arrived in excellent condition, but was soon eaten.

She wrote about house problems, both for herself and for our parents:

How is the house situation? I think you are right that your present difficulties will always recur at more or less frequent intervals at 5PP [Pembridge Place], and I'm sure in the long run you wouldn't regret moving to a smaller comfortable modern house—though the actual moving would be horrid. Go to Highgate or elsewhere where the air is fresher, and the sky bluer, than in North Kensington. Have a few good-sized rooms and lots of comfortable arm-chairs, thick walls, large windows and a white-tiled kitchen. If you want to make a fortune, or alternatively to be kind to your friends, keep 5PP and let it as flats.

Pembridge Place had been a nagging problem for some time. Even in her fourth year at Cambridge Rosalind had written:

> You've heard most of what I think about returning to 5PP many times before. London, yes—excellent idea. But you'll never again be able to run that house satisfactorily, least of all now. If, as mother says, it needs 3 maids, you won't get them, and if you could you oughtn't to.

(This was before the days of dishwashers and other modern domestic gadgets.)

For Rosalind, after a time the gloomy dusty room and the gloomy landlady became depressing. She decided she could stay in Paris only if she found somewhere better to live. 'If a miracle happened and I got a flat here,' she told Colin, 'I might feel like staying longer, but I'm pretty fed up with this room.' Eventually, early in 1950, she did find 16 Avenue de La Motte Piquet 7me, a flat with a telephone (previously there had only been the possibility of receiving calls in a very public telephone in Mathieu's office, or queuing endlessly in a post office to make one).

Feeling that with a flat she could happily stay in Paris a few more years, she was hopeful:

> It's not ideal, but I think it's better than this—and of course much more expensive. It's a furnished flat, the snag being that I share it with a young American couple—he to work in our lab. There are 2 bedrooms, drawing room, salon and a rubbish room which will serve as a spare bedroom for anyone not too fussy, plus kitchen (small) and 'cabinet de toilette' with a heatable shower but no bath. None of the rooms is big, but all but the

FIG. 19. 16 Avenue de la Motte Picquet in Paris, where Rosalind shared a flat (photo Simon Glynn).

dining room are bright and pleasant. They have the dining room. The salon, next to my bedroom, is much the nicest room, and so they have to have access to it. I don't know quite how it will work out, but I shall normally eat in the salon and they'll use it when they have guests and if they're in in the day-time and I hope not much otherwise—I shall promptly spread my things about it as much as possible…As for the Americans, he is very pleasant and easy to get on with. She is a bit more difficult, but means well and I think it will work out all right…The district here is, of course, much less attractive than my old one, but that is the only real change for the worse. I'm about twice as far from my work, but on a direct bus route—it takes 25–35 minutes...Here we have central heating controlled <u>inside</u> the flat—an excellent system, and the American carries the coal up the six floors from the cellar.

There are plenty of danger signals in that letter. Successful sharing needs space, and the idea of sharing a small kitchen with an unknown wife of an almost unknown colleague was tricky. And it is interesting to note that Rosalind, not much of a feminist in her approach here, expected the husband to carry the coal, and the wife to share the kitchen. There was no security of tenure, because the owner, in the army in Germany, had the right to reclaim the flat at two months' notice. But the flat was, on the whole, a pleasure, in spite of occasional friction. She was not there for long; in less than a year she was to move back to London.

In her first surviving letter home from the Avenue de la Motte Picquet, in February 1950, Rosalind said she was 'beginning to feel almost settled in and almost to get fond of this place'. It was further from the lab, but

the time I waste in travelling I more than save in not walking along miles of cold corridor to the kitchen and not lighting a fire and huddling over it to get warm in cold weather.

Transport strikes, she noted, 'will be more nuisance for me personally now than before, as I am twice as far from my work'.

A hurried letter in March 1950 explains she has to prepare two papers for a meeting at the Sorbonne, so 'I've got to re-read and re-learn stuff that I produced a year ago. My first impression on re-reading it is that it's rather good but very largely new to me.'

It wouldn't be easy to leave Paris, particularly now that she had at last got a flat—or at least half a flat. Her letters show that she had been constantly under pressure from our family to come back, and she constantly and patiently explained that she would come in time, but that she must finish the (unspecified) work she was doing. 'As long as I've got work to do here and no job in London I'll stay here':

> Of course I agree that I must not stay here indefinitely, though I've already been here long enough to realise that it will be difficult to leave—much harder than leaving London to come here, because the break will be more permanent. I came here on a visit but my life remains largely centred in London, but when I move back I shall be leaving people and places for good.

She had looked at labs in London on her visit in January 1949 (a year before she found the Paris flat), with a view to moving for the academic year in October, though nothing came of it. She had not been surprised when she was turned down at Birkbeck—she was, as it happened (though she didn't know it), in good company, for Francis Crick was also turned down for a job at Birkbeck that year. 'Anyway,' she wrote, 'my work here is going extremely well and it would really be a pity to drop it at the moment. Getting a job should be easier when it is published.' So, with a promising flat and flourishing work she would, as she wrote in June 1950, have been happy to stay another year.

But the decision had been made by November 1950, when she assured our parents:

> It has always been clear to me, and I think I have always made it clear to you, that my one and only reason for returning to London is that the family and perhaps the greater part of my friends are there. It is, of course, an important reason— sufficiently important, in fact, to get me back to London in spite of my preference for Paris, the French way of life, the mass of French people and (not a negligible factor) the Parisian climate.

This may well have been true, but it was not really the whole truth. It leaves out the question of the future direction of her work, which was immensely important to her. According to the historian of science Robert Olby, she 'began to feel that she ought to get back into the British scientific community before it became too difficult to make the return'. Vittorio Luzzati tells me that the distinguished crystallographer Dorothy Hodgkin had advised her that the time had come to make up her mind whether to come back to Britain or to settle in France. She had originally intended to spend only about two years in Paris. This had extended to four, although our parents had constantly begged her to come back; she would only do so if an appealing job appeared.

She knew that, although she had not then been accepted at Birkbeck, there were new opportunities and possibilities in London. In 1949, on her visit home, she had seen Charles Coulson at King's College, and the following year she had sent him a copy of her letter to the journal *Nature* on her work and had asked his advice about ICI Fellowships, which could be held at various universities:

> It's not a particularly distinguished thing to apply for [she wrote home], and doesn't lead to anything particular (it lasts 3 years) but if the work available pleases me it would be all right. So far I don't know anything about the work, so that even the half of me which is open-minded about it can't yet decide whether it wants it or not.

Charles Coulson was Professor of Theoretical Physics at King's, and she had come across him in her BCURA days, when he himself had been an ICI Fellow. We of course didn't realize until much later what a fine reputation she already had at that time for her carbon work, and how much she had achieved in Paris. Not only had her letters never discussed her papers, but the term 'X-ray' had never even appeared.

In June 1950 she had an interview for the Fellowship, telling our parents that she was disappointed, rather than flattered, to be summoned:

> I should really like one more year here—this would be the time to decide whether to stay longer or not. In any case if I get the thing this year I should have a shot at getting it postponed till Jan 1st.

She did get 'the thing', and did postpone it till the new year.

Coulson was encouraging and steered her in the direction she was to follow for the rest of her life. 'If you are interested in possible biological applications of the technique that you now know so well,' he had written to her, 'there could be quite a lot to be said in favour of King's.' 'I am, of course, most ignorant about all things biological,' Rosalind confessed, 'but I imagine most X-ray people start that way. I am certainly interested in the biological X-ray work.' She felt ready for a new challenge. The new techniques she had learnt in Paris, under Mering's guidance, for the study of the microstructure of carbons, were about to be applied, with conspicuous success, to the study of DNA.

CHAPTER 8

Misery in London

Rosalind was awarded a Turner & Newall three-year Fellow-ship, similar to the ICI Senior Postdoctoral Fellowships, to start at the beginning of 1951. She was not altogether pleased to be supported by an industrial firm, though this was well before the days when asbestos, and Turner & Newall as its main producer, became notorious. At that time Turner & Newall, like ICI, was a flourishing company using some of its profits virtuously to support basic research.

It was not easy to leave Paris, 'leaving people and places for good'. Rosalind had been happy, had loved the place and her life there. Ever sensitive to her surroundings, and feeling a need for light and open air, she was depressed by the prospect of a war-scarred London and a lab 'in a cellar' instead of windows looking out over the Seine. She may have found the political scene more encouraging in England, where the Labour Party filled the gulf between the dangerous extremes of communism and what she saw as the fascism of de Gaulle, but she would not have welcomed Churchill as a peacetime prime minister.

She wrote to Colin:

My feelings about moving from here still oscillate wildly. When I left London I thought I'd almost convinced myself it wasn't too bad, then when I got back and saw Paris and cycled to work all along by the Seine I was miserable. At the moment I'm feeling more reconciled.

My personal assistant is most touchingly heartbroken. A few other people are genuinely sorry, more are politely sorry, and one or two, I suspect, may be pleased.

And she wrote home:

In summer it is particularly hard to contemplate changing the banks of the Seine for the Strand. Air and sunshine make such a big difference to life…This summer I've been going out into the country nearly every fine Sunday with the Luzzatis—and here nearly every Sunday is fine—cycling or swimming…Now, having told you all about our nice climate, I must plunge out into torrential rain to buy some food.

She had voluntarily and definitely made the decision to move, though she was full of doubts and found it hard to accept:

I still spend at least half my time wondering—very seriously—whether to chuck up the whole thing and stay here. If I could postpone it a year I shouldn't hesitate—but I can't. Equally, if I had succeeded in creating for myself a wider circle I shouldn't hesitate to stay on indefinitely—while liking the mass of people around me very much, my intimate circle remains small. It isn't so much a question of London or Paris as of England or Europe. I like Europe and the Europeans so much better than England

and the English…All this is not new in me, but dates at least from my early Cambridge—or even late St Paul's days.

London in the 1950s seemed to Rosalind to be sunk in pessimism, while Paris, recovering from the horrors of occupation, was forward-looking and full of optimism. She had analysed this view in a letter written while on holiday in France, possibly as early as 1946 (though she hardly ever put the year on letters). The French recovery from the war, she thought, was amazing:

> Almost everyone I have met has spent the war in hiding, some with false papers, has lost numerous close relatives and friends, mainly by deportation, and has lost most of his belongings. But their concentration on the present enables them to start a new life, however different from the old, and to be wholly in it. If France had been inhabited by Englishmen in 1940 the disintegration would certainly not have occurred. But if the English had suffered during the war as the French did and if the life of individuals had been so profoundly changed, then the English would still be thinking about their sufferings and yearning for their former life instead of so readily starting afresh.

Drab and war-scarred, London was not the multinational city that it has now become. Rosalind might have been readier to accept the move today, when a third of the population of London is foreign-born, new buildings have covered the bomb-sites, and new laws have abolished the smog. In the French-speaking lab in Paris, she had enjoyed the company of her very international colleagues—she had been working under Mering, who, it turned out, was a White Russian, while her best friends were the Luzzatis (who had arrived in Paris just after her), one Italian and the other French in origin, but both from Argentina. 'I wish', she wrote unrealistically, 'I knew of a job that would keep me at least half the year in Paris and the rest in London.'

It was not a good mood for the start of a major move, a new life, and a new job. She had gone eagerly to Paris, full of hope; she came back to London wary and full of doubts. To turn it all into a happy success, King's would have to be friendly and welcoming, the work would have to be stimulating, and she would need somewhere encouraging to live. The last two conditions were fully met, but the whole project was nearly wrecked by the failure of the first.

Her introduction to King's was in no way friendly or welcoming. The atmosphere in some of the labs, with what Brenda Maddox has called their 'barracks-room beer-drinking camaraderie',[1] was sadly different from anything Rosalind had been used to in Paris. There were certainly a surprising number of women scientists at King's, but they were not allowed in the men's common room, where there was lunch and coffee and contact with colleagues—an insulting situation, even if not unusual in England at that time; it hit Rosalind particularly badly after the freedom and friendliness of the lab in the Quai Henri IV. And the immediate hostility between Rosalind and her colleague Maurice Wilkins has become notorious.

Occasional breaks brought pleasure, but coming back was always hard. In June 1951, after only a few months at King's, she was off to the big crystallography conference in Stockholm; in August she was in Brittany; and at Christmas she was back in Paris wondering whether the whole move back to London had been a mistake and consulting Vittorio Luzzati about the prospects of giving it all up and going back to Paris.

In Brittany Rosalind spent some time with a group of French friends, and then moved on to join her school friend Anne who, with her husband and small children, had rented a derelict farmhouse near the Lascaux caves. 'Rosalind flourished in the freedom of a holiday like that,' Anne wrote in her reminiscences. 'She was kind, generous, relaxed and always at her best with children. That is how I remember her.'[2]

Rosalind escaped again several times in 1952, first to North Wales for an Easter holiday with Margaret Nance, who seems to have accepted Rosalind's attitude to walking and mountains; then in May her coal research work brought her a very welcome invitation to Yugoslavia, where she lectured, travelled, and made new friends. Her work-based visit to Ljubljana included a holiday in a villa by the lake in Bled; the father of her colleague there was a senior member of the Slovenian Academy, and this entitled him, and three generations of his family and their friends, to spend their holidays there:

> We went up for three and a half days of real mountains, in the Julian Alps, staying in mountain huts and going up Triglav, the highest mountain in Yugoslavia (about 9,500 ft). It was lovely to be back among mountain tops again, for the first time in 5 years. Our way down led through 'the valley of the Seven lakes', which is a National Park because of its botanical and zoological interest. I have never seen such a wonderful spread of Alpine flowers—both high up on the rocks and scree and lower in the valley there was far more variety and colour than I have seen in France or Italy.

In Bled, she had enjoyed the company, impressed at 'what a civilised life they manage to lead with almost no money at all'. Then she moved to Kotor, where her host, gynaecologist for the district, forbade pregnant women to ride bicycles 'with the result that we can easily borrow bicycles from his patients, which provides a good way of going along the sea-level roads on either side of the fjord'.

Rosalind had a holiday in Italy too that summer, with Elisabeth Reinhuber, a friend of Colin's wife Charlotte. Elisabeth wrote to me in 1996, with vivid memories of Rosalind and of the trip they had had forty-four years earlier:

> We walked into Rome through the gate nearest the Piazza del Popolo, and I remember so distinctly her 'Isn't this glorious'. We moved through Naples across the Sorrento peninsular to the then dream-place of Palinuro—she had marked it as being furthest away from the railway line. We walked down towards it from the little station in the hills and people asked us on the way, surprised, whether we had relatives down there. We did a lot of walking and swimming—she had a little metal box for four raw eggs to suck for energy.

But these breaks can only have added to Rosalind's unsettled feeling, and made life at King's seem even less tolerable. It was the unhappy side, her doubts, and her personal misery, that we, her family, saw. We were hardly aware of the excitement and achievement of her work. She had told Coulson that she knew no biology, but she soon became totally immersed in the deoxyribonucleic acid (DNA) problem, understanding the importance of the new challenges and what she could contribute.

As she herself had written, when discussing her abortive research project in Cambridge, 'to do any work that is worth while one needs to be passionately interested in one's subject'. And she tackled the problem with enthusiasm.

She had come back for her work, but also, as she had told our parents, for her family and friends. We had left Pembridge Place by then, and moved to Hocroft Road, a much less interesting neo-Georgian house at the edge of Hampstead, complete with central heating, water accessible from a comparatively modern kitchen, and a large garden. Still, Rosalind had been on her own, with short gaps, ever since Cambridge, and there was no question of her moving back. She was lucky to find a flat in Drayton Gardens, on the edge of Chelsea, just off the Fulham Road. It was not a very grand flat in a not very grand block, but it was purpose-built, warm, she could entertain her friends there, she didn't have to share it, and she loved it. She had a reasonable-sized living room, with a picture she was fond of—windswept trees on a hillside—and her framed photographs of mountains. Her furniture, as far as I remember, was comfortable rather than elegant— a convertible sofa, an armchair, a small Victorian dining table and chairs. The bedroom had the beautifully made walnut chest of drawers that my father had given her—he had a liking for good craftsmanship. There was also a bathroom, a separate lavatory, and a kitchen where, if you sat on a stool up to the worktop, there was just room to have breakfast. It was near shops and a cinema. It was also near my father's sternly feminist sister, our Aunt Alice, who was proud of her distinguished niece and endlessly kind to her. Rosalind was to stay in this flat for the rest of her life, and it now boasts the plaque commemorating her DNA work.

She was generous with the flat, lending it to friends when she was away. Anne Sayre has described how, when she borrowed it, she found it thoughtfully stocked with food Rosalind knew she liked. At another time, in her own absence, Rosalind set it up to cater for her friend Mair Livingstone with her newborn baby. The flat must have helped Rosalind to feel more settled.

But in spite of the pleasure and independence of her flat, the two famous years of her life (the years of the DNA research at King's) were scientifically exciting but socially miserable—both to an extent greater than she could have expected. Much has been written about this period, and without it she would long ago have been forgotten by nearly all except her family and friends; but it was only a two year period. The original plan was that she was to work on the structure of proteins in solution, but she was asked by Professor John Randall, the Director of the Biophysics Research Unit at King's, to use her skills to investigate 'the structure of certain biological fibres' which would, he said, be 'more immediately profitable and perhaps fundamental'.[3] In fact, therefore, it was Randall who directed her to the DNA problem. His letter gave her the impression that she would be in charge of the work—a point that Randall failed to explain to Maurice Wilkins, who was away on holiday at the time. At a meeting in his office in January, Randall introduced Rosalind, passing Raymond Gosling on to her as a Ph.D. student. Gosling, recruited by Randall, had previously been working under Wilkins, who says he himself suggested that Gosling, with some experience of X-ray diffraction, should work with Rosalind in future—'the PhD slave boy handed over in chains', as Gosling later cheerfully explained to Anne Sayre. What Wilkins had not suggested was that Rosalind, who he had thought would be his assistant, would be in charge of the DNA research, which he considered to be his own province. But that was what he found when he came back from his holiday.

So the relations between Wilkins and Rosalind started off badly, and never recovered. Temperamentally, too, they were almost bound to irritate each other, with Rosalind's quick direct manner conflicting with Wilkins' slow deliberateness. Matt Ridley, in his life of Francis Crick, wrote that Wilkins was 'semi-silent', with 'meandering conversation (usually delivered at an angle of ninety degrees from the listener)';[4] Brenda Maddox describes him as, at this time, 'just this side of eccentric'.[5] And Rosalind was never good at accommodating herself to anyone she found uncongenial. The clash, because of the importance of the work they were involved in, has become appallingly famous. It was a pity, Brenda Maddox wrote, that Rosalind never tried to make peace by inviting Wilkins to dinner at her flat; but it was she who was the newcomer, and he certainly never invited her, in spite of prompting from his Jungian analyst who thought it might help the prickly relationship. Wilkins had, apparently, been consulting a Jungian analyst about his own uncertainties for some years, long before Rosalind arrived, after a failure to find any help from a Freudian.[6]

Rosalind got on well with Raymond Gosling, her research student, but otherwise felt unhappy and isolated. In fact it was only with Raymond Gosling that she could carry on the kind of impassioned arguments about her work that she had enjoyed with Vittorio Luzzati and would enjoy later with Aaron Klug. As Gosling said, in an interview with Anne Sayre:

If you believed what you were saying, you had to argue strongly with Rosalind if she thought you were wrong, whereas Maurice would simply shut up. He wouldn't really go out on a limb and justify himself…Rosalind always wanted to justify herself, or, if she was discussing with me, she always expected me to justify myself very strongly indeed. And of course I found this a tremendous help. I learned a lot from her that way.[7]

Rosalind desperately needed to sharpen her wits against a colleague, not to have him 'simply shut up'. Crick and Watson both gained enormously from bouncing ideas off each other. Rosalind had only her research student.

If only Rosalind and Maurice Wilkins had been able to cooperate, if only they had been able to argue out the problems together—the whole DNA story is full of 'ifs'. Wilkins, in his memoir *The Third Man of the Double Helix*, blames Randall (whom he admired in many ways) for telling Rosalind that he was handing the DNA problem over to her. 'If Randall had not barged in it might even have been that Rosalind could have worked happily alongside Stokes and me, and her professional X-ray approach could have combined fruitfully with our techniques and theorising,'[8] he wrote rather patronizingly. Superficially, Maurice Wilkins had much in common with Rosalind; they were both educated at Cambridge, were politically left wing, had relatives who had been involved in the women's suffrage movement, had parents who had encouraged them by equipping workshops at home—the name 'Maurice' had even been given in homage to her father's hero, Frederick Denison Maurice. But Wilkins hated argument. Rosalind was 'very fierce, you know', he told Anne Sayre, 'She denounced, and this made it quite impossible as far as I was concerned to have a civil conversation. I simply had to walk away.'[9] It was completely the wrong reaction. Resentment built up on both sides—where there shouldn't have been sides at all—and Rosalind beavered away on her own.

In spite of all the difficulties the beavering was wonderfully productive. Her work provided crucial information that led to the discovery of a structure that would suggest likely and simple answers to fundamental questions of reproduction and inheritance, in a way that no one had foreseen.

It has been clear from time immemorial that the offspring of living organisms tend to resemble their parents, and by the nineteenth century the only plausible explanation of that resemblance was that a great deal of information is transmitted from one generation to the next in the eggs or sperm, or pollen grains or spores, or whatever. How the information is stored and how it is used were complete mysteries. In the 1850s and 1860s, however, Gregor Mendel's work on hybrid peas showed that the inheritance of individual characteristics often follows rather simple patterns, and that those patterns gave important clues to the way the information is packaged and handled. An important finding was that, when a hybrid is the offspring of parents differing in a particular trait, each individual egg or pollen grain produced by the hybrid has information about only one of the two parental traits. In other words, the information about a particular feature received from the two parents is segregated in the formation of the eggs or pollen grains that will pass the information on to the next generation. Mendel wanted a word to describe the instructions that could be used to produce a particular trait, and he called it a 'differentiating element'—we now call it a gene. What it was physically remained a mystery.

The next step was finding the location of genes. Chromosomes—bodies found in the nuclei of dividing animal and plant cells, and readily stained by basic dyes (hence their name)—were discovered in the middle of the nineteenth century but their function was unknown. Early in the twentieth century, though, Theodor Boveri in Würzburg and Wayne Sutton in Columbia University pointed out the resemblance between the segregation of traits discovered by Mendel, and the separation of chromosome pairs in the formation of eggs and sperm. This was suggestive; but overwhelming evidence linking a variety of genes with particular chromosomes was discovered by Thomas Hunt Morgan in experiments on fruit flies (*Drosophila melanogaster*) at Columbia University. At last, Mendel's differentiating elements were linked to particular objects.

The third step was to ask: What are genes made of? By the 1930s it was known that chromosomes consist mainly of proteins and nucleic acids. Because proteins are made of twenty different kinds of amino acid, exist in many different forms, and are capable of a great variety of functions, whereas nucleic acids are made of only four kinds of subunit and were thought to have a monotonous structure, it was widely assumed that it is the proteins that store genetic information. This view was changed dramatically by a paper published by Oswald Avery and his colleagues at the Rockefeller Institute, New York, in 1944. Remarkably, this paper was entirely concerned with pneumococci, the bacteria responsible for pneumonia, and it arose from an observation made by Frederick Griffith, a medical officer in the Ministry of Health in London, thirteen years earlier. What Griffith found was that something from heat-killed pneumococci of one strain could change the nature of living pneumococci of another strain so that they had all the properties of the first strain—including the ability to produce generation after generation with these properties. Unless one believes in resurrection of the dead, the heat-killed pneumococci must contain some 'transforming principle' that converts the living bacteria from one strain to another. Avery was determined to discover what this transforming principle was, and after four years of hard labour he and his colleagues succeeded in showing that it was DNA. The problem, then, was: How is DNA able to store vast amounts of genetic information, and to make that information available for further use? Answering that problem required knowledge of the structure of DNA.

Rosalind's challenge was to tackle this structural problem, applying the new techniques and the skills she had learnt in France. But she was not only a superb experimentalist, getting important results from her practical skills. As Aaron Klug explained, in a talk opening the new Rosalind Franklin Design, Technology and Engineering Workshop at St Paul's School in 1984, 'coupled with her practical skills was a powerful mind, and it is this combination which made her such a successful scientist'. She thought about the problems, designed her own experiments, realized what really mattered.

In 1993 the Dictionary of National Biography issued a 'Missing Persons' volume to assemble biographies of those who had been ignored at the time of their death or who 'had acquired posthumous fame'. In it Aaron Klug wrote this summary of Rosalind's work:

> Within the first year Franklin transformed the state of the field. She produced much better X-ray patterns, and, by introducing methods to control and vary the water content of the specimens, she was able to show that the DNA molecule could exist in two forms (A and B), and to define conditions for the transition between them. In May 1952 she obtained the superb patterns of the B form which now [as 'photo 51'] grace the text books, and which J D Watson saw early in 1953. Inspection of this helical pattern, together with the distribution in December 1952 of a report by Franklin of her work, gave crucial information to Watson and F Crick for the final building of their DNA model in February–March 1953.[10]

The drier A form, being crystalline, gave X-ray diffraction patterns of greater clarity but, unlike the B form, these patterns did not obviously point to a helical structure. Because of their clarity, however, Rosalind spent a large part of 1952 investigating the A form, before she turned her attention again to the B form.

The 'inspection' of the famous 'photo 51' (which had been taken in May 1952) was made in January 1953 by Watson, who had been shown it by Wilkins without Rosalind's knowledge. As Watson correctly wrote later, 'Rosy, of course did not directly give us her data', but he went on to say, quite incorrectly as far as the photo 51 was concerned, 'for that matter, no one at King's realised they were in our hands'.[11] The information in Rosalind's report, written for the Biophysics Committee of the Medical

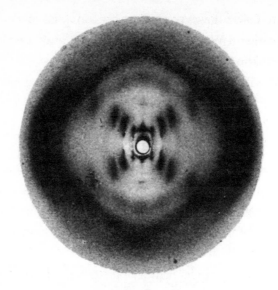

FIG. 20. 'Photo 51'.

Research Council, was in a slightly different situation. In fact it discussed matters that Watson could have gathered, but failed to understand, when he heard her paper at the King's Colloquium in November 1951. Remembering, wrongly, Rosalind's account of the water content of the samples, he had built a model which, as she pointed out as soon as she saw it, was impossible and was not compatible with her results. Max Perutz, as head of another Medical Research Council unit, the unit for Molecular Biology, had seen the report but being, as he later admitted, 'inexperienced', did not consider it confidential, and showed it to Crick and Watson. He wrote later in the journal *Science* that it contained no data that 'Watson had not already heard about from Miss Franklin and Wilkins themselves. It did contain one important piece of crystallographic information useful to Crick; however, Crick might have had this more than a year earlier if Watson had taken notes at a seminar given by Miss Franklin.'[12] Yet another 'if' in the story.

But Rosalind never did know that Watson had seen either the 'photo 51' or her report, and that she had thus unwittingly provided Watson and Crick with the crucial information they needed. Had she known what had been going on behind her back and with no acknowledgement, her fury would have been understandable and alarming. As it was, she was impressed, and not at all angry, when she saw the final model—though she must have been sorry that she herself had not quite got there. Not surprisingly, it fitted her results.

Watson's first model had been a shameful failure, but even before Crick and Watson, with the benefit of the new information, produced the final stunningly successful model, Rosalind had made the decision to move because of her unhappiness at King's. She had been well on the way to discovering the structure herself, though anxious, perhaps over-anxious, to be quite certain of her results before publishing them or experimenting with models. She had not been racing the Cambridge group, but did have something of a personal race, to complete as much of her work as she could before her move to Birkbeck in the middle of March 1953. Her typescript summarizing her results, which Aaron Klug later found and analysed, was actually dated 17 March—just one day before the news of the Watson-Crick model reached King's.

In his 2004 article for the *Oxford Dictionary of National Biography*, Klug wrote about this typescript draft, showing how far Rosalind herself had got towards solving the structure:

FIG. 21. Quentin Blake drawing of Rosalind with Crick and Watson and a Double Helix (reproduced by kind permission of Quentin Blake).

The draft contains all the essentials of her later paper (with Gosling) in *Nature* in April, together with one by Wilkins and his colleagues, which accompanied Crick and Watson's paper announcing their model for the structure of DNA. In Franklin's draft it is deduced that the phosphate groups of the backbone lie, as she had long thought, on the outside of the two coaxial helical strands whose configuration is specified, with the bases arranged on the inside. Her notebooks show that she had already formed the notion of interchangeability of the two purine bases with each other, and also of the two pyrimidines. The step from base interchangeability to the specific base pairing postulated by Crick and Watson is a large one, but there is little doubt that she was poised to make it. The notebooks also show that she had grasped that the A form contained two chains or strands which ran in opposite directions, but had not understood the exact relation between the two forms.[13]

There is a final 'if' from Wilkins, justifying himself and wondering whether they could have collaborated rather than quarrelled: 'She did not mention the idea of base-pairing; but I was keen about the importance of that idea, and if she and I had discussed the problem there would have been little to prevent us finding the Double Helix.'[14]

Crick himself wrote that 'Rosalind would have solved it…with Rosalind it was only a matter of time'.[15]

Interestingly, a recently discovered letter sent by Crick to Wilkins on 5 June 1953 (two months after the DNA structure had been published in *Nature*), suggests that as well as benefiting from seeing 'photo 51' and Rosalind's report to the Medical Research Council Biophysics Committee, he and Watson also benefited by NOT having seen the photograph of the diffraction pattern of the crystalline A form of DNA which Wilkins had just shown them:

> This is the first time I have had an opportunity for a detailed study of the picture of Structure A, and I must say I am glad I didn't see it earlier, as it would have worried me considerably.[16]

This was the crystalline form, yielding diffraction patterns of great clarity but not obviously pointing to a helical structure, that had distracted Rosalind in 1952. Once the structure had been solved, she was criticized for spending so long on the A form, but this letter helps to explain why she did so.

I should like to be able to say I remember the excitement of the DNA work, but I'm afraid that would not be true. Elisabeth Reinhuber, 'untutored and unknowledgeable about natural sciences', writes of one day when Rosalind 'said with some fervour "I think I have found something rather exciting"', but she does not say when or what that was. Similarly, I have a memory of a train journey, when a graph gave her an unexpected and exciting answer, but I can't remember what it was all about. I feel sympathy for her friend Ann Piper who wrote: 'I remember our being in her flat one evening and churning away on a hand calculator to produce some of the results. She would show me her patterns with great pride, but I never had the remotest idea of the enormous importance of the work she was doing, nor did I appreciate the great significance of her achievements.'[17] The same is true of the press reaction, or lack of it; as Matt Ridley has written, 'It was a momentous spring: Everest climbed, Elizabeth crowned, Stalin dead, *Playboy* born. The biggest event of all—life solved—caused barely a ripple.'[18] Except among a very few scientists directly involved, it does not seem to have been a 'eureka moment'. Robert Olby, who was to write *The Path to the Double Helix* in 1974, said in his preface, 'I cannot recall the word DNA even being mentioned when I was a student at London University in the early fifties'.

Even in April 1953, with the publication of the classic DNA papers in *Nature*, Rosalind very seldom talked to us about her work. I think we were more aware of Rosalind's unhappiness than of the triumph of the project. Our main feeling was pleasure that she was moving to what promised to be a happier lab. There were major distracting domestic events in the family that year too—each of my three brothers had a new baby, so our parents may have been more concerned with being grandparents than with the structure of DNA. There are no letters from Rosalind to them from this time because, living in her flat in London, she would see them nearly every weekend. Her laboratory notes, written in school notebooks, are now in her archive at Churchill College, Cambridge.

Rosalind left the misery of King's in March 1953 and moved, with the third year of her Turner & Newall Fellowship, to Birkbeck. Randall, furious, added to his reputation for appalling personnel management by writing, a week before the famous three papers on the structure of DNA appeared in *Nature*:

> I appreciate that it is difficult to stop thinking immediately about a subject on which you have been so deeply engaged, but I should be grateful if you could now clear up, or write up, the work to the appropriate stage.[19]

And, he added, she should no longer supervise Gosling.

These orders were neither sensible nor possible. How could she, at such an exciting and critical time, stop thinking about the subject? And how could she desert Gosling, who had worked cheerfully and well with her for the last two years? So the orders were ignored and Gosling thanked her, and her alone, in the introduction to his thesis. And while her apparatus was being prepared at Birkbeck, she had time to prepare a paper giving further evidence in support of the Watson–Crick model, the first analytical demonstration of its correctness,[20] which appeared, with Gosling as joint author, in *Nature* in July. But, as Max Perutz pointed out later, 'Rosalind Franklin's immediate

and generous provision of the experimental evidence supporting the structure did not prevent Watson from presenting her
as the ogre of the discovery.'[21]

Shaking off the dust of King's, Rosalind typically decided to
take a long journey before settling down to her new problem at
Birkbeck. This time, breaking new ground, she decided to visit
scientists and family connections in Israel, travelling with Anne
Piper as far as Ljubljana where they visited Rosalind's familiar
scientific colleagues; Anne remembered one telling her 'she
makes my clockwork tick'. Impressed by the Israeli scientists,
and feeling happy and at home with various friends and relations, Rosalind was appalled by the extreme orthodox Jews and
their way of life, and shocked at the brash attitudes she found in
Tel Aviv. At the Weizmann Institute: 'I find more of interest and
more people ready to talk interestingly than in any lab I've ever
visited…From a purely scientific point of view I should be very
tempted to seek work here—for the climate too, which at
present is wonderful—but it is socially a far too small and isolated community.' It was a strange contrasting society, and it
worried her.

CHAPTER 9

Viruses, Models, and Success

Rosalind left King's, with some relief, in 1953, and moved to Birkbeck, famous for the distinguished virus department run by Desmond Bernal.

Bernal was a pioneer of X-ray crystallography and a man of immense knowledge—he was generally known as 'Sage'. His two drawbacks were his extreme left-wing views—he remained a communist and supporter of the Soviet Union even through the Lysenko affair[1] and through the Soviet invasion of Hungary—and his endless pursuit of endless women. Rosalind managed to ignore both these sides of his life, and simply to admire him as a great scientist. Marcel Mathieu, a communist, had been her boss in Paris, and she was now to have a communist boss in London. I remember her telling me with pleasure about the mural Pablo Picasso, a fellow communist, had drawn in Bernal's flat at the top of 22 Torrington Square. Her lab was next door, at 21 Torrington Square, both of them rather attractive, crumbling Georgian buildings belonging to London University and both now demolished (though the Picasso has been saved, and is now owned by the Wellcome Trust). The lab was at the top of the house, in the servants' old quarters, five floors up from her X-ray equipment in the basement—an arrangement that was tiring at the best of times; mildly amusing at first, it became increasingly wearing and distressing as her illness progressed.

For the remaining five years of her short life she worked on the structure of viruses, with the tobacco mosaic virus as the main example. It might seem strange that Rosalind, who hated being involved in industry, should not only be supported by a big asbestos firm, but should also devote her energies to investigating a virus that damaged the tobacco plant and thus the tobacco trade. But the tobacco mosaic virus had a fundamental importance that went far beyond anything its name might imply.

Its story went back more than fifty years. Maurice Beijerinck, the microbiologist son of a Dutch tobacco dealer who had been bankrupted by the mosaic disease, was anxious to research the cause of the problem. Building on earlier work by Adolf Mayer and by Dmitrii Ivanowski, he found that when the sap of an infected plant had been filtered to remove all known bacteria, the resulting liquid was still infectious and even produced further infectious fluid when it was injected into a healthy plant; what is more, infection only occurred if the injection was into a part of the plant containing dividing cells.[2] The infective agent, smaller than any bacterium, was clearly something important to investigate. Beijerinck named this infective agent 'a virus' (from the Latin word for a poison); it was the first virus to be discovered and it became the prototype for investigating virus structure. Working out that structure, and the relevance of the structure to the virus's reproduction, was a challenging and fundamental problem. Rosalind's new approach and new techniques might be crucial. In an unsuccessful effort to make our parents understand what she was doing, she bought them a Pelican book by F. M. Burnet, *Viruses and Man,* but plant viruses only get a passing mention in it, and they didn't manage to tackle the book anyway.

Bernal himself, with Isidore Fankuchen, had done some X-ray work on the tobacco mosaic virus in the 1930s, and James Watson had investigated it more recently—in the brief period when DNA work had been banished from the Cavendish. Rosalind was one of the next in this distinguished field, confidently building up a splendid and harmonious team, with Aaron Klug (later a Nobel Prizewinner and President of the Royal Society) as a colleague, and with Ken Holmes and John Finch (both later Fellows of the Royal Society) joining them in 1955 as their research students. The American biophysicist Don Caspar, over in Cambridge for a year, joined them for a time.

Paris had been wonderful but, we always thought, temporary; King's had been exciting but unhappy; now it seemed as if Rosalind had a promising job she enjoyed, back in London with her own flat, and with very congenial colleagues. The pattern of her life seemed secure.

While Rosalind was at Birkbeck there were again no letters to our parents (because she was in London) but there was a series of very full letters from her two journeys to America. The navy had taken Colin across the Atlantic to the West Indies, and had taken Roland to Canada, but none of us had been to

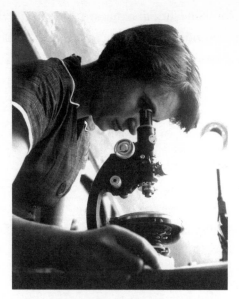

FIG. 22. Rosalind with microscope.

the United States and so we were particularly glad to get Rosalind's impressions.

Her first invitation to America was to a Gordon Conference on coal, in New Hampshire in 1954. This was when, as she wrote home, her Paris work was so highly appreciated. Aged thirty-four and independent, she was, all the same, still writing home every week when she was away, and expecting weekly letters back. Brenda Maddox rated this series of letters as 'a fine contribution to the tradition stretching from de Tocqueville and Fanny Trollope to Alistair Cooke'.[3] But Rosalind was not writing for publication; these letters were simply a diary of events and reactions, written for family consumption. 'In spite of her seeming independence,' as my mother wrote, 'for her the family was very close, and her major concerns incomplete without their sympathy and interest.' Here is her first letter after arrival, dated 15 August:

> We are about 100 people living in the school in a fairly remote and green part of the country [in New Hampshire]. Naturally I find myself making endless generalisations about America and Americans from this non-representative sample of each...The overwhelming impression so far is of overabundance of every-thing, and the resulting complete self-confidence of individuals. I think the confidence is responsible for most of their virtues and their vices. It makes for easy, friendly social relationships, which are pleasant but only rarely more than superficial. It makes the American bore more insufferable than any other bore I've ever met...The district is becoming rapidly depopulated because it's not rich enough to support the American standard of living. I find myself pointing out that there's something wrong in the world when land like this is being abandoned while strenuous efforts are made to cultivate the desert and the jungle in other and less temperate regions...The more I hear of the scale of American scientific research in money and men, the more I'm impressed by the superiority of Europeans, who continue to contribute a large proportion of the fundamental work...I enjoy this place, though I shall be quite glad to move on and see more of America, and visit the scientists who interest me more—those in subjects related to my present work.

She had no praise for American food—tasteless, she reckoned, and only redeemed by the supply of sauces or jellies and pickles.

A week later she was in Boston after an eventful visit to the Marine Biological Station at Woods Hole, where she had stayed with 'a somewhat eccentric family' with eight children under fourteen, who told her, without anyone really believing it, that there had been a hurricane warning. It was a strange experience, but there were no casualties and it was not really violent enough to be frightening:

> The wind had been strong all night. When I first went out, about 9 a.m., the wind was lifting large amounts of sea and blowing it across the village, and the water level, 3 hours before high tide, was already well above the high tide level...Soon we saw from the laboratory windows that piers and landing stages were breaking up. Then the water came up over the sea wall—just rising steadily, with a rough sea but not really giant waves. Cars parked in the lower part of the town began to get wet and there was a rush to find high parking places. I came home to see how things were in my digs and found water half way up the walls in the sitting room, and the older children proudly told me that they'd been giving their younger brother a swimming lesson...There was an endless succession of strange sights...In fact it was exactly like the pictures that one sees of heavy floods but doesn't really expect to become involved in.

Woods Hole was full of scientists from all over America, as it always is in summer. This time it included James Watson, who discussed tobacco mosaic virus with her, and even suggested she should join him and Sydney Brenner in a drive across to California, but she was committed to lectures on coal in various cities before she could go West. She met him again in California.

The next surviving letter is to Colin and his wife Charlotte. She found the reactions to the hurricane to be 'matter-of-fact and English', far calmer than she expected. She wrote to them about the workers in her own field, fundamental biology, where America, she found 'is really leading':

> They have a remarkable number of first class people among the under 30s. In spite of the vast distances, they all know one another well, and constantly exchange visits. These people impress me very much in many ways—personal, scientific and political.

Like many English visitors, she enjoyed Boston and felt at home there. It is curious, in view of her earlier opinions about the 'boringness' of England, to see the appeal of this most English of American cities. She was unwilling to leave it for her formidable schedule of travel:

> There have been so many new impressions in this small corner of the country that I'm quite frightened by the thought of all that there'll be to absorb once I really start travelling around. I spend the week-end in New York, then fly to Pittsburgh & Penn State College & back to N.Y. the following week, then go across by stages to California. I now hope to include Washington on my way back from California.

Boston, she wrote home, was the best of American cities, but New York was the worst. She did enjoy the New York skyline though:

> The sky-scraper group, from the distance, is surprisingly beautiful, and changes with changing light like mountain scenery. I have to keep telling myself that it's real.

Pennsylvania State College appalled her—'devastatingly dull'—and Pittsburg was dirty, with nearby blast furnaces pouring out smoke. But, after all, she was there for carbon talks. A weekend with the Sayres was compensation; she had met David, a crystallographer, in Paris, had enjoyed the company of his wife Anne there and at the crystallography congress in Stockholm in 1951, and was happy to be with them again after three years, 'just wandering around and talking, looking at the museum, staring at fish in the aquarium, and eating Anne's excellent food'. Rosalind was always appreciative of interesting food, especially after her first experiences in America.

The carbon part of her visit ended in Chicago ('my 8th and last talk'), to her relief—'the carbon crowd are entirely uninspired, but in the biological laboratories there are an impressive number of really first-class people'. In this same letter, seventeen months after the famous *Nature* papers announcing the structure of DNA, she wrote that 'in the biological laboratories I have much to learn and almost nothing to give'.

The best part of staying in Chicago was being among friends:

> Coming to the Ellis's [Evi's parents] on Monday evening felt almost like coming home. Conversation is rather as though they were just members of the family who have been away rather a long time.

Then she travelled West, stopping on the way for a proper tourist visit on a mule in the Grand Canyon. 'Highly coloured and impressive,' was her verdict, 'but not nearly as beautiful as real mountains.' Then she stopped at Pasadena, on her way to Berkeley:

Scientifically the Pasadena visit was most interesting and enjoyable, and here at Berkeley it promises to be quite as good. If things go on all right at Birkbeck (and I don't know quite definitely, till I get back, whether I've got my contract for the next three years or not) my work will certainly benefit from this journey in a way which could not have been achieved without personal contacts. Apart from the value of discussions, I've found a number of good people willing to send me material to work on.

But Berkeley, on this first visit, turned out to be a mixed blessing, in spite of its famous virus laboratory, headed by Wendell Stanley and including Fraenkel-Conrat and Robley Williams:

The surroundings are beautiful, the climate perfect, and San Francisco is almost a civilised city. But it was the first unfriendly lab I've come to. The visit was very interesting and important for me, but was entirely formal although it lasted 4 days, and 4 out of 5 evenings I was simply returned to my hotel at 5.30. I don't know the explanation, but the contrast with all the other places I've been to was striking. On the Sunday I was, however, driven around San Francisco Bay and got my first really clear view of the Pacific, which was exciting. We watched a mass of pelicans over the sea, and saw a golden eagle inland.

Washington, with friends from the Woods Hole hurricane, was friendlier, and she was duly impressed with its elegance.

She came home by sea on the *Liberté*. Having money left over from her grant, she baffled the Coal Board by trying to return it.

Back in London, Rosalind had an amiable correspondence with Watson, following their meeting at Woods Hole, on the problems of tobacco mosaic virus[4]—further proof of her ignorance of how her DNA results had been used without her knowledge. There is also a letter, dated 18 July 1955, to a colleague at the University of Wisconsin, that implies that Watson was not widely known at that stage: 'Jim Watson (of the DNA model) is back in Cambridge…between us we want to look at as many viruses as possible.'[5] She showed total lack of resentment against the Cavendish team; Aaron Klug has said that he never heard her complain about Crick or Watson, but she simply had great admiration for them. Quite a strong friendship grew between her and the Cricks, particularly with Francis Crick's half-French wife, Odile.

All projects, even the most promising ones, have their problems. For the Birkbeck tobacco mosaic virus project, the cause of the problem was disagreement with the virologist Norman Pirie, leading to a severe financial crisis. Pirie was the famously clever head of the biochemical department of the Agricultural Research Station at Rothamsted, a Fellow of the Royal Society, a member of the Agricultural Research Council, and a powerful man in the field; in 1936 he had succeeded in crystallizing the tobacco mosaic virus. He was sure—too sure—of his own beliefs, and scornful of Rosalind's conflicting (and, as it turned out, correct) results which she reported in a letter to Nature in 1955.[6] Pirie wrote her an abrasive letter of criticism: 'As you probably expected, I have all the usual objections to this paper,' he began, 'but in case the faults have slipped in through inadvertence I may as well itemise some of them. You start off with a bald erroneous statement',[7] and so on. Not a nice letter to get from someone who was high-powered and had influence with your paymaster. Rosalind defended herself politely, adding rashly, 'I hope that you do not disapprove so strongly of what

I have written that you will never again be willing to provide us with material to work on.'[8] Maybe she had given him the idea, but this is exactly what he did do. Even worse, through his friendship and influence with Sir William Slater, the Secretary of the Agricultural Research Council which was supporting her research after the final year of her Turner & Newall fellowship, funding for her and for the whole group was in danger.

So it was difficult to get herself and her group onto a sound footing. Her own salary, as she pointed out firmly in a letter to Bernal, was, because of unexplained meanness from the Agricultural Research Council, less than the average received by physicists of her age.[9] She was not in any way grasping, but she resented unfair treatment. It was two years after the publication of the DNA structure, but William Slater still refused to give her the grade of Principal Scientific Officer on the grounds that, at her age, it would be 'only for the exceptionally distinguished'.

There are reports and notes of meetings that show continual frustration and lack of appreciation. Slater told her in September 1955 that it was unlikely her group could continue in London, that she (but not the rest of the group) might move to Cambridge (where, as she pointed out, there would be no workshop facilities for her), and that he strongly disapproved of her working on 'second-hand material'—a reference to her highly successful collaboration with colleagues at Berkeley and Tübingen, who, not equipped to use X-ray diffraction to carry out structural studies themselves, had sent virus derivatives for study. An extra insult was that she should work under the constant guidance of a biochemist, so that she could understand the biological implications of her work. She wanted a biochemist in the team, but not to supervise her. Slater would not discuss the question of Aaron Klug's future, saying there was 'plenty of time', seeming to have no understanding of the need for thinking ahead.

In this crisis, with Aaron Klug's fellowship about to run out, there was a new idea, the possibility of help from America. Rosalind had met Robley Williams, professor in the department of virology at Berkeley, the previous year on her visit to California; she admired his work, and he knew hers. Now coming to Birkbeck on a site visit, seeing its lack of basic equipment, and hearing about all the problems, he suggested that it might be worth applying to the US National Institute of Health. It was. Rosalind had not thought that an American institution would support a British research project, but in March 1956 she wrote a further report on her research group, presumably (though there is no heading in the copy in the Churchill College archive) for the US National Institute of Health, explaining the need for equipment and forward planning, emphasizing the importance of the work she was doing on viruses, and, incidentally, showing how it linked with her work at King's:

> The work is concerned with what is probably the most fundamental of all questions concerning the mechanism of living processes, namely the relationship between protein and nucleic acid in the living cell. It is known that the nucleic acids carry genetic information, and that they are intimately connected with the synthesis of proteins. While a considerable amount is known about the molecular structure both of the nucleic acids and of proteins, almost nothing is known of the *in vivo* relationship between the two types of molecule...Although the work is at

present being done exclusively on plant viruses, there is no doubt that a large part of the results obtained will also be relevant to the problems of animal viruses...In no other laboratory, either in this country or elsewhere, is any comparable work on virus structure being undertaken.[10]

She concluded that:

Making some allowance for steadily rising costs, and excluding the requirement of a biochemist, the annual cost of maintaining in Birkbeck College a research group which could efficiently apply itself to the study of the fundamental problems of virus structure would be of the order of £10,000 p.a.

In the spring of 1957, before she had a response from the National Institute of Health, she was told by the Agricultural Research Council that they would renew her grant—but only for £4,300 and only for one final year, ending in March 1958. Fortunately, in April, she heard that her application to the National Institute of Health had been entirely successful: she was promised the full £10,000 a year for three years. This was more than anything Birkbeck had received before—Aaron Klug says the Master of Birkbeck College thought there was to be a total of £10,000, not an annual payment.[11] Even though the personal salaries for Rosalind and Aaron were beaten down by the Master to the minimum, the group was safe for the next three years.

In the same month that she wrote the report, she gave a paper[12] at the CIBA Foundation Symposium on the Nature of Viruses, a small conference that included, by invitation, her DNA associates Crick, Watson, and Wilkins as well as the

'TMV men'—Klug, Caspar, Robley Williams, and Pirie. In this paper she described an important advance in knowledge of the structure of the tobacco mosaic virus. Nearly two decades earlier, Bernal and Fankuchen had shown that the virus consisted of identical protein subunits. By 1955 it was known that all viruses consist of both protein and either DNA or RNA (ribonucleic acid); in 1952 Watson had shown that the protein subunits in the tobacco mosaic virus were arranged in a spiral, and in 1955 Don Caspar, in his Ph.D. thesis at Yale, showed that there was a hole down the middle of the spiral.[13] What Rosalind and her group reported was striking X-ray-diffraction evidence that the RNA (probably a single molecule) winds around the inside of the central hole, in a helical groove between the protein subunits.

Shortly after the CIBA conference, the virus scientists reassembled at a meeting in Madrid. It was Rosalind's first visit and, in spite of her objection to Franco and all he stood for, she went, and toured round Spain afterwards with the Cricks.

The next American trip followed, this time funded by the Rockefeller Foundation, to a Gordon Conference on nucleic acids, much more to her taste than the one on coal. On the way, she went first to a conference 'attended by an overwhelming array of great names' at Baltimore, and then stayed with the Sayres in New York. The Gordon Conference itself was full of people from the labs she wanted to visit; afternoons were free, so there was plenty of time for hill-walking and lake-swimming. There was more swimming, and more meetings with scientists later, in a weekend at Woods Hole—'here biologists from all over the world come for the summer, and those who stay long

bring their families, so it's a happy mixture of serious laboratory work and seaside resort'. She was to stay a few days with
Mamie's niece Rachel Shavit and her scientist husband in Madi-
son, and again with the Ellis family in Chicago, but otherwise
her plans were wonderfully open—flying to Los Angeles for a
week divided between two groups of labs, then back to Berkeley
where Heinz Fraenkel-Conrat was working with Robley
Williams on tobacco mosaic virus, and possibly another week
or two somewhere else.

The visit to Rachel was more dramatic than expected, with a
sudden storm blowing up while they were sailing on the lake:
'As we got back to the shore it was raining moderately hard and
the wind was quite strong, but we thought it was all rather a
fuss. However, 5 minutes later there was such a rain as I have
never seen, and bits of trees were blowing across the road.'
Rosalind's second experience of violent American storms. She
found Rachel's six-year-old son was, in spite of parental opposition, keen on playing with toy guns, telling her that 'in Israel
when I grow up I first have to go into the army, there we have
real guns, and America sends guns to every country in the
world'.

She had a thoroughly enjoyable time at the University of
California, Los Angeles (UCLA), and 'completely fell for South-
ern California, not only because of a really wonderful mountain trip'—though that must have helped. She was impressed
by fine new houses, equipped with workshops where the
owners even made some of their furniture, because *'everybody*
earns a lot, so nobody can afford to pay anybody else'. As for
the trip:

After 2 days at UCLA I was driven over to the California Institute of Technology—'Cal Tech'—about 25 miles away. Here the person I had written to [identified by Brenda Maddox as Renato Dulbecco] asked whether I was more interested in mountains or in the ocean. I didn't like to say straight out that there was nothing I would like more than to be taken up a big mountain, so I just said 'mountains'. Further questions followed at intervals during the first day of lab visits. Would I mind spending a night out in the mountains? Would I like to walk for just about 2 hours to look at a lake? Would I be prepared to carry things a little way so that we didn't have to sleep right by the car? Finally four of us set off at 6 a.m. on Friday...by 11 a.m. we had driven the 220 miles to a point 8,500 ft high at the foot of Mt Whitney (14,495 ft), the highest point in the USA (outside Alaska), and were walking upwards carrying sleeping bags, blankets, and food for 24 hours. It's no good trying to describe mountains, they all sound the same, but this was incredibly beautiful, and got consistently and amazingly more beautiful as we went up—huge trees, alpine flowers and small lakes, huge rocky crags with quite a lot of snow remaining, and a wide view of the desert behind us...Perhaps the most remarkable moment of the trip was opening my eyes at dawn to see the great rocky mountain straight in front of me, with its thin pink line of sunshine along its summit.

We got down to the car about 10 a.m. and were washed, dressed, and talking viruses in the lab by 5 p.m.!

After this, Berkeley (in spite of the support she had had from Robley Williams) seemed as unfriendly as before:

Everybody seems to wonder why I have come, and to behave as though I hadn't—apart from an English couple from Cambridge, here temporarily. It is probably the biggest and most important virus research establishment in the world, but both as a unit and as individuals they take themselves far too seriously. But I think I am managing to collect some useful material to work on when I get back.

She worked with Fraenkel-Conrat there for three weeks on heavy metal derivatives of TMV, the technique that had recently been pioneered by Max Perutz in his work on haemoglobin. Back in Birkbeck, she used this technique in the work praised by Bernal in his obituary, 'combining the study of the intact virus with that of a reconstituted virus without nucleic acid and using substituted mercury atoms as markers'.

There is no mention in her letters home of the pains that started while she was in California. A doctor gave her painkillers, and advised her to see someone as soon as she got back, but she did not take the warning seriously enough. In fact she postponed her return by a week. Her colleague Don Caspar had not been able to come to Berkeley because his father had just died, so Rosalind went to see him at his home in Colorado, and then planned to go once again to Woods Hole and to New York. Would it have helped if, instead of ignoring her pains, she had gone into a hospital in California for investigation, or had rushed straight home? It's impossible to say.

Rosalind saw doctors as soon as she was back in England. Ovarian cancer was diagnosed, and she began the terrible alternations of operations and treatments and hopes. (Incidentally, the fact that Rosalind sometimes stayed with the Cricks or with my brother Roland in the convalescent stages of her illness is sometimes cited as evidence of bad feeling between her and our parents. It was not that at all; she had found our mother's obvious concern and distress hard to bear.)

The achievements of her group had outward forms that even our family could appreciate. In the summer of 1957, already ill, Rosalind at last had public triumph, making models of the viruses she had been studying, and showing them at the Royal Society's summer *Conversazione*. Our parents, to their pride and delight, were invited to a formal lecture by Robley Williams at the Royal Institution shortly afterwards, where two models she had made with Aaron Klug were on display and there were admiring references to her work. Lawrence Bragg, who had impressed his students with her models in his recent lectures, asked her to produce a giant version of the tobacco mosaic virus model, about five feet high, to be shown at the Brussels World's Fair in 1958.

Model-building involves ingenuity, often with the use of most unlikely materials. Rosalind planned this model in the intervals of her illness, first using the entire stock of bicycle handlebar grips from the local Woolworths. I remember taking an architectural model-maker to see her to discuss the problem when she was in University College Hospital, and my brother Colin remembers, on a brief walk while she was recovering from an operation, that she spotted polystyrene moulds in the window of a shop displaying hats; immediately realizing that masses of similar polystyrene moulds were just what she needed, she went in and asked whether they could supply 250! Rosalind did not live to see the Fair, but the model, with its array of polystyrene units, was a dramatic exhibit, and later was to find a prominent home in the new Molecular Biology Building in Cambridge.

FIG. 23. Model of Tobacco Mosaic Virus, made for Brussels World Fair 1958 (photo Medical Research Council Laboratory of Molecular Biology).

Between hospital stays, she went back to the lab. In her last summer, making the most of the little time she had, she travelled to Italy with me in the open Morris Minor I was proud of, and I am mortified to find she described the journey disparagingly as 'travelling around in a little tin box', for it was not her traditional style of travel. My father told me to make it as good a holiday as I could for Rosalind, as it would probably be her last.

We all knew the diagnosis only too well, but kept a wild hope that some miraculous cure might be found. Rosalind herself believed that if she could last another five years something might have been discovered. Now, more than fifty years on, the prognosis for ovarian cancer is still poor. Rosalind struggled on for another twenty months, optimistically planning a new research project, complete with a three-year research grant from America, this time on the structure of the polio virus. I remember that one day she brought home a sealed and well-wrapped thermos to be kept in our fridge overnight, cheerfully explaining to my mother that it contained live polio virus; she was taking it to safe storage at the London School of Hygiene and Tropical Medicine rather than in the ancient crumbling buildings of Birkbeck. At that time polio was much in the news—Werner Ehrenberg, the physicist at Birkbeck who had developed the X-ray equipment Rosalind used, had suffered from it himself, and it was only in the previous year that Jonas Salk's vaccine had been licensed; Albert Sabin's oral vaccine was not licensed until 1962. Rosalind was just starting her polio work when she died, on 16 April 1958. It was left for Aaron Klug and John Finch to take over and decipher its structure.

There was a brief obituary in *The New York Times*,[14] one by our uncle Norman Bentwich in *The Jewish Chronicle*, and one by Bernal in *Nature*.[15] Bernal, to the family's pride, also wrote a fine obituary in *The Times*; first writing of her carbon researches, and then of the work at King's, he went on to describe her work at Birkbeck:

Miss Franklin took up the study of what is probably the most thoroughly studied of the plant viruses—that of Tobacco Mosaic disease—and almost at once, using the techniques she had already developed, made notable advances in it. She first verified and refined Watson's spiral hypothesis for the structure of the virus. She then made her greatest contribution in locating the infective element of the virus particle— its characteristic ribose nucleic acid. This she did by combining the study of the intact virus with that of a reconstituted virus without nucleic acid and using substituted mercury atoms as markers. Thus she was able for the first time to set out the structure on a molecular scale of a particle which if not in the full sense alive is capable of the vital functions of growth and reproduction in other cells.[16]

In 1962 Aaron Klug moved, with Ken Holmes and John Finch, to the new Medical Research Council Molecular Biology Laboratory in Cambridge. Had she lived, Rosalind would have moved back to Cambridge with them.

CHAPTER 10

Afterlife

Bernal wrote a fine obituary, St Paul's School and Newnham wrote nothing. 'Her work on viruses was of lasting benefit to mankind' is the simple wording inscribed on her tombstone. True, of course, but remarkably to modern eyes there is no mention of DNA. Some have asked for the inscription to be changed, to be brought up to date; but in fact it marks a moment in history—April 1958—before DNA had become familiar letters, and before Rosalind's name was known outside the scientific community. Crick and Watson got their Nobel Prizes in 1962, without mentioning Rosalind in their speeches. Scientists were aware of the omission, the general public was not, and there it might have remained had it not been for Watson's book, *The Double Helix*. Symbolically, Rosalind first appeared in the *Dictionary of National Biography* in the short article by Aaron Klug in the *Missing Persons* volume (1993); he was able to write a fuller article in the 2004 *Oxford Dictionary of National Biography*.

The Double Helix was, and still is, highly successful and highly readable. But it is more of a novel than a factual account, unfair to Watson's colleagues, and particularly unfair and hostile to Rosalind. It appeared in 1968, ten years after her death, fifteen years after the famous papers had been published in *Nature*, so the idea that it has the truth of immediacy is doubtful. The book was not so much Wordsworth's 'emotion recollected in tranquility' as emotion romanticized—what Watson would like people to think he remembered. Readers of the book are given no idea that Rosalind became a friend of Francis and Odile Crick, even travelling round Spain with them after the conference in Madrid, or indeed that she and Watson had later amiable conversations and correspondence about virus structures.

We, her family, were of course unhappy about the book, but we were not the only ones—there is a five-page strongly worded letter, written by Francis Crick on 13 April 1967, begging Watson not to publish: 'Anything which concerns you and your reactions, apparently, is historically relevant,' he wrote, 'and anything else is thought not to matter. In particular the history of scientific discovery is displayed as gossip. Anything with any intellectual content, including matters which were of central importance to us at the time, is skipped over or omitted. Your view of history is that found in the lower class of women's magazines.' Unfortunately, many have always accepted it as real history. The book, Crick added, 'grossly invades my privacy',[1] for he felt that nothing personal should be written about him in his lifetime. (You may think that quoting this letter invades Crick's privacy, but he copied it to ten others at the time; and he is no longer alive.)

Crick does not mention Rosalind in his objections, any more than either he or Watson had mentioned her or her work in their Nobel Prize speeches; this seems to have been a deliberate policy as, planning the speeches with Watson, Crick had written that 'personally I am against anything in the way of a historical account of this work'.[2] He wrote a similar letter to Wilkins (who, in the event, did make a brief reference to Rosalind's 'very valuable' contribution). Crick had, however, written to the French biologist Jacques Monod in December 1961 that 'the data which really helped us to obtain the structure was mainly obtained by Rosalind Franklin'.[3] (Though, as Robert Olby has written in his recent biography of Francis Crick, 'Crick was as sensitive to issues of priority and borrowings as anyone else when he felt he was the victim'.[4])

My father had died in 1964, four years before the book appeared, but my mother, who lived until 1976, felt that she would rather Rosalind and her work were forgotten than that she should be remembered through Watson's eyes. She would have been happy and proud if she had known what followed. First (and she did know this) Rosalind's American friend Anne Sayre decided to write a book in Rosalind's defence—a protest, as she said, that Rosalind could no longer make herself. *Rosalind Franklin and DNA* is not such a successful and readable book as *The Double Helix*, but after thirty-five years it is still in print. It was the start of what has become something of a 'Rosalind industry'.

Anne Sayre, among others, has objected to the nickname 'Rosy' that Watson uses in his book, but the nickname, even if only used behind her back, doesn't bother me. We had a Great Aunt Rosy and, as it happens, a Great Aunt Jenny, both of them small and both wearing black velvet bands round their necks.

One minor incident about Great Aunt Rosy and Rosalind comes to mind, trivial but illustrating both Rosalind's shyness as a child, and the grandeur of Chartridge. Rosalind went to the lavatory one night, and heard Aunt Rosy announce at breakfast that she had heard footsteps; scared to say it was only her, Rosalind was ever more scared as the problem escalated and she never did confess, even when the alarm grew until the police were called to watch the house. As for Great Aunt Jenny, I am told that Colin, aged six or so, told her that I was not to be called 'Jenny', because it was a horrible name. Anyway, Rosalind and I both had to make do with only the first syllables of our names, and became Ros and Jen in the family.

What does bother me, and bothered Anne Sayre, is the picture of Rosalind as an unattractive belligerent bluestocking, churning out results secretively and without understanding, a warning to girls who might be thinking of a career in science. In reaction, this was followed by the picture of a neglected woman scientist, 'the forgotten heroine of the race to unravel the mystery of human DNA' as The Observer picturesquely put it in 2002. It is hard to say how far her difficulties at King's were added to because she was a woman, as well as arising from a basic personality clash, but it suited the feminism of the sixties and seventies to show her as a victim of male dominance, and to trumpet her achievements as the triumph of a woman in a man's world.

So now, as a result of The Double Helix and of the attempt, conscious or not, to airbrush out Rosalind's contribution to the DNA story, Rosalind's fame has continued to grow, in a way that would have astonished and embarrassed her, and that still baffles members of her family. It is certainly no longer true that she is 'the forgotten heroine'. And she was never a feminist—she would have thought of herself simply as a scientist whose achievements should be judged on their own terms, not as a 'woman scientist' striking a blow for the rights of women. Watson's portrait of her may have made some worried parents see her career as a warning, but in reaction they now see her as triumphing against all the odds, and put her on an unrealistic pedestal. Many parents in Britain and in America now hope her career will inspire their scientific daughters.

There are endless websites for 'Rosalind Franklin' on the Internet. Some of these are wildly inaccurate, like the one that says she was the only girl in a family of four, and many repeat the myth that my father was opposed to her going to university or studying science; much the best is the site produced by the National Library of Medicine, USA, for their 'Profiles in Science' collection.[5]

In 2003, the fiftieth anniversary of the announcement of the Watson-Crick model was marked by meetings and articles on both sides of the Atlantic, and by a subsequent rash of memorials to all concerned, including Rosalind. Brenda Maddox, one year earlier, had written the well-known biography of Rosalind, with a full account of the part she played in the DNA story; King's, doing its best to make peace and to proclaim its achievements, has given her name to a distinguished series of lectures, and now boasts a Franklin–Wilkins Building on its Waterloo campus, while a whole university has adopted her name in Chicago. More than compensating for earlier neglect, Newnham named its new graduate block the Rosalind Franklin

Building (1995), and St Paul's School built its Rosalind Franklin Technology Centre (1984)—converting the old swimming pool where Rosalind had taught me to swim on 'little sisters' days' after school. I must add how pleased my parents would have been by the panels of distinguished alumni outside King's in the Strand, which show Rosalind alongside Frederick Denison Maurice, the founder of the Working Men's College where my father gave so much of his free time and his talent.

Laboratories and halls named after her are scattered over the country, in the Genome Centre in Cambridge, in Birkbeck, in schools—I keep on coming across more. There have been plays, projects for films, television features—notably the BBC TV *Horizon* programme in 1987, with Juliet Stevenson playing the part of Rosalind, as well as the British and American DNA commemorative programmes in 2003. It still goes on, with a new play by Exeter University students at the Edinburgh Fringe, and another in New York, both in 2010 and both called *Photo 51*. Perhaps the memorials that would have pleased her best are those that use her name to promote opportunities for young academics—the annual award given by the British government in association with the Royal Society to promote women in science, technology, engineering, and mathematics, and the fellowships given by Groningen University to help launch women who are beginning their academic careers.

After Rosalind's death, Aaron Klug, who had worked with her at Birkbeck but had not known her during her time at King's, studied her King's notebooks to trace the progress of her research. He published his conclusions in two articles in *Nature*,[6] and in the 2003 celebrations in Cambridge he gave a historical survey of the DNA story, how 'the structure was solved in the Cavendish Laboratory, Cambridge, by Francis Crick and James Watson, using X-ray diffraction data from fibres of DNA obtained by Rosalind Franklin at King's College, London'. As he said in the epilogue to his talk, the discovery of the structure was the beginning of the molecular biology of the gene.[7]

So Rosalind became a symbol, first of an argumentative swot, then of a downtrodden woman scientist, and finally of a triumphant heroine in a man's world. She was none of these things, and would have hated all of them. She was simply a very good scientist with an ambition, as she told Colin from her hospital bed, to be a Fellow of the Royal Society before she was forty. But she died at thirty-seven. She would have liked the letter, written to me in 2002 by Peggie Cronin, a maid in our house at the outbreak of war, who had gone to her book group to hear a talk about the Maddox biography:

Dear Mrs Glynn, [she wrote] although I can only think of you as little Jenifer, I couldn't believe my ears when I realised that Rosalind Franklin was one of the family of 5 Pembridge Place by whom I was employed in 1939.

NOTES

Chapter 2

1. Letter from Helen Bentwich to her husband Norman in Palestine, 22 August 1926.
2. Gwen Raverat (1952), *Period Piece*, Faber & Faber, p. 58.

Chapter 3

1. Hypo is the fixer, not the developer; but Colin's account of Rosalind's reaction stands.
2. Jean Kerlogue (née Kerslake) (1993), memories of Rosalind, manuscript sent to Colin.
3. Five good grades in 'school certificate', the earlier equivalent of GCSE, were needed for 'matriculation', before a candidate could be considered by a university.

Chapter 4

1. Cambridge, Newnham College Archive, Franklin Papers, folder 2, Gertrude Dyche (née Clark), MS note.
2. Cambridge, Newnham College Archive, Franklin Papers, folder 3, Delia Agar, MS comments on Anne Sayre's book, 1979.

Chapter 5

1. The quotation is from an article about R. G. W. Norrish written by Frederick Dainton and B. A. Thrush (1981), in *Biographical Memoirs of Fellows of the Royal Society*, pp. 379–424.

Chapter 6

1. R. E. Franklin (1949), 'A Study of the fine structure of carbonaceous solids by measurements of true and apparent densities. Part I: Coals', *Transactions of the Faraday Society*, 45, 274–86.
2. P. J. F. Harris (2001), 'Rosalind Franklin's work on coal, carbon and graphite', *Interdisciplinary Science Reviews*, 26, 204–10; H. C. Foley (1995), 'Carbogenic molecular sieves; synthesis, properties and applications', *Microporous Materials*, 4, 407–33.
3. R. E. Franklin (1949), 'A Study of the fine structure of carbonaceous solids by measurements of true and apparent densities. Part II: Carbonised coals', *Transactions of the Faraday Society*, 45, 668–82.
4. Jean Kerlogue (née Kerslake) (1993), memories of Rosalind, manuscript sent to Colin.

Chapter 7

1. Armin Hermann, 'Max von Laue', in *Dictionary of Scientific Biography* (1970–80), Scribner's, New York.
2. The quotation is from 'Rosalind Franklin Papers: The Holes in Cole Research at BCURA and in Paris, 1942–1951'. *Profiles in Science*, website produced by National Library of Medicine, USA.
3. Aaron Klug (2004), 'Rosalind Franklin', in *Oxford Dictionary of National Biography*, Oxford University Press.
4. 'Rosalind Franklin Papers: The Holes in Coal', *Profiles in Science*, website produced by National Library of Medicine, USA.

Chapter 8

1. Brenda Maddox (2002), *Rosalind Franklin*, Harper Collins, p. 128.
2. Anne Piper (née Crawford) (1998), 'Light on a Dark Lady', *Trends in Biochemical Sciences*, 23: 151–4.
3. Cambridge, Churchill College Archives, letter from Professor John Randall to Rosalind Franklin, 4 December 1950.
4. Matt Ridley (2006), *Francis Crick*, HarperPress, p. 52.
5. Maddox, *Rosalind Franklin*, p. 138.
6. Maurice Wilkins (2003), *The Third Man of the Double Helix*, Oxford University Press, pp. 112–13, 150.
7. Anne Sayre (1975), *Rosalind Franklin and DNA*, W.W. Norton, p. 103.
8. Wilkins, *The Third Man*, p. 149.

9. Sayre, *Rosalind Franklin*, p. 105.
10. Aaron Klug (1993), 'Rosalind Franklin', in *Dictionary of National Biography: Missing Persons*, Oxford University Press.
11. James Watson (1968), *The Double Helix*, Weidenfeld & Nicolson, p. 181.
12. Max Perutz (1969), 'DNA Helix', *Science*, 164, 1537–9.
13. Aaron Klug (2004), 'Rosalind Franklin', in *Oxford Dictionary of National Biography*, Oxford University Press.
14. Wilkins, *The Third Man*, p. 221.
15. Sayre, *Rosalind Franklin*, p. 213 (interview with Crick).
16. A. Gann and J. Witkowski (2010), 'The Lost Correspondence of Francis Crick', *Nature*, 467: 519–24.
17. Piper, 'Light on a Dark Lady', 151–4.
18. Ridley, *Francis Crick*, p. 73.
19. Cambridge, Churchill College Archive, Franklin papers Box 1, section 3, Letter 17 April 1953 from Professor John Randall to Rosalind Franklin.
20. Aaron Klug (2004), 'The Discovery of the DNA Double Helix', *Journal of Molecular Biology*, 335, 3–26.
21. Max Perutz (1981), 'Undercurrent of revelations (Review of *The Double Helix*, ed. G. S. Stent)', *New Scientist*, 26 March, p. 827.

Chapter 9

1. Lysenko was director of Soviet biology; he rejected Mendel's views, and, with Stalin's support, insisted on an agricultural policy which proved disastrous.
2. M. W. Beijerinck (1898), 'Concerning a contagium vivum fluidum as cause of the spot disease of tobacco leaves', In English (1942) in *Phytopathological Classics*, no. 7, pp. 33–52. American Phytopathological Society, St Paul, MN.
3. Brenda Maddox, *Rosalind Franklin*, Harper Collins 2002, pp.243–4.
4. Cambridge, Churchill College Archive, Franklin papers section 3 letters dated 7 March 1955 and 10 June 1955.
5. CCA, Franklin papers section 3, Letter from Rosalind Franklin, to a colleague in Wisconsin, 18 July 1955.
6. R. E. Franklin (1955), 'Structure of tobacco mosaic virus', *Nature*, 175: 379–81.
7. CCA, Franklin papers section 3, Letter from Norman Pirie to Rosalind Franklin, 6 December 1954.

8. CCA, Franklin papers section 3, Letter from Rosalind Franklin to Norman Pirie, 7 December 1954.

9. CCA, Franklin papers section 3, Letter from Rosalind Franklin to Desmond Bernal, 25 July 1955.

10. CCA, Franklin papers section 4, Rosalind Franklin, *Note on the future of the ARC research group in Birkbeck Crystallography Laboratory*.

11. Aaron Klug, video interview recorded on website webofstories, 2005.

12. R. E. Franklin, A. Klug and K. C. Holmes (1957), *CIBA Foundation Symposium on The Nature of Viruses*, pp. 38–55, 'X-ray diffraction studies of the structure and morphology of tobacco mosaic virus'. See also R. E. Franklin (1956), 'Location of the ribonucleic acid in the tobacco mosaic virus', *Nature*, 177: 928–30.

13. D. L. D. Caspar (1956) 'Radial density distribution in the tobacco mosaic virus particle', *Nature*, 177: 928.

14. *New York Times*, 20 April 1958.

15. Desmond Bernal (1958), Obituary of Rosalind Franklin, *Nature*, 182: 154.

16. *The Times*, 19 April 1958.

Chapter 10

1. London, Wellcome Library, PP/CRI/I/3/8/4, Letter from Francis Crick to James D. Watson, 13 April 1967.

2. London, Wellcome Library, PP/CRI/A/3/1/2, Letters, 30 October 1962.

3. London, Wellcome Library, PP/CRI/H/3/5/1, Letter from Francis Crick to Jacques Monod, 31 December 1961.

4. Robert Olby (2009), *Francis Crick*, Cold Spring Harbor Press, p. 147.

5. profiles.nlm.nih.gov/

6. Aaron Klug (1968), 'Rosalind Franklin and the Discovery of the Structure of DNA', *Nature*, 219: 808–10 and 843–4; Aaron Klug (1974), 'Rosalind Franklin and the Double Helix', *Nature*, 248: 787–8.

7. Aaron Klug (2004), 'The Discovery of the DNA Double Helix', *Journal of Molecular Biology*, 335: 3–26.

INDEX